SHOWCASE OF INTERIOR DESIGN™

PACIFIC EDITION

Vitae Publishing, Inc.
Grand Rapids, MI

■

Library of Congress
Cataloging-in-Publication Data

Showcase of interior design /
[edited by Mary Jane Pool].
— Pacific ed.

p.   cm.
Includes index.
ISBN 0-9624596-3-1: $35.00
1. Interior decoration—California—Pacific Coast—History—20th century.
I. Pool, Mary Jane.
NK2004.S54   1992   728'   .09794—dc20   92-3500   CIP

■

VITAE PUBLISHING

CHAIRMAN—JOHN C. AVES
PRESIDENT—JAMES C. MARKLE
Midwest Publisher—Gita M. Gidwani

■

PACIFIC EDITION PROJECT STAFF

Publishing Director—Phillipa M. Gettman
Publishing Coordinator—Sheri L. Rambaud
Marketing Coordinator—Lisa K. Webb
Editorial Coordinator—Pirrie B. Aves
Greater Los Angeles Publisher—Bret Parsons
Greater San Francisco Publisher—Jack L. Clark
Arizona/Southern California Publisher—Gail Hayes Adams
Associate Publisher—Francine E. Port

■

AVES INCORPORATED

Art Direction—Carol Dungan
Production Artist—Nancy Allen
Production Supervision—Douglas Koster
Inquiry Management—Jill Nabozny
Financial Management—Robert Spaman

■

USA distributor to the trade:

Watson-Guptill Publications
1515 Broadway, New York, NY 10036

International distributor:
Rockport Publishers, Inc.
P.O. Box 396, Five Smith Street,
Rockport, MA 01966

Printed in Singapore by Toppan
Typeset in USA by Vitae Publishing, Inc.

■

Title Page Interior Design: Wes A. Hageman, ASID
Photo: David Glomb

ACKNOWLEDGEMENTS

■ *Michelangelo said, "If people knew how hard I work to achieve my mastery they wouldn't think it was so wonderful at all." Great talent and genius often seem to rise out of nowhere, because great people usually operate with such seemingly effortless grace. This is nowhere more evident than in the field of design.*

The caliber of designers whose professional practice has taken them to the levels described in this resource book work hard. Most have studied formally, all have studied exhaustively. Their education includes practical matters of safety, comfort and durability as well as the theory of color, design history, fabric and furniture manufacturing. The professional in the design service industry also commands knowledge and control of the little details that can destroy a great concept, such as insurance and shipping. Said Carlyle: "Genius is the capacity for taking infinite pains."

The value in retaining a designer's services is found in this full range of skills. They do not expect to be paid for just laying under a tree, gazing up into the blue sky, and waiting for an inner explosion of inspiration. Creativity is hard work and the execution of a plan can be torturous. If one is contemplating a decorating project that will provide long lasting value, comfort and satisfaction, a hard working genius is the answer. We know our readers will find many such paradoxical surprises in this edition of Showcase of Interior Design. ■

John C. Aves

TABLE OF CONTENTS

4

■

In This Climate Of Change What Is The Next Design Trend, And, Should We Really Care?

Recently I heard someone on television say that "everything good starts in California." Did not catch what they were referring to, but it reminded me that the West Coast is where so many of the best ideas in architecture and design have started. There always seems to be a fresh current of change coming in from the West.

The climate and dramatic setting have produced a way of life, more relaxed and closer to nature, that has swept the nation. The rush began when air conditioning became a perfected science. Bungalows, saltboxes and colonial houses were opened up with walls of glass. Nature moved into big spaces that were once a series of small rooms. Loggias and porches were glassed-in for living closer to the garden, greenhouse kitchens and spa baths developed to bring the outdoors in. Wherever we live we want to approximate the almost totally outdoor lifestyle of the western part of the country.

The pounding Pacific, the rugged coast from Alaska to Mexico, the titanic mountains, the green valleys, the sandy deserts, and the giant rivers have inspired a design mood that is big and expansive. Now we reach for a sense of "big space" and "big scale." We want big window walls; big-scale furniture, soft and cushiony; big slabs of stone, wood, and other great natural materials incorporated into our houses. We want the works of artists influenced and nurtured by the dramatic landscapes of the West. An architect once said to me, "Michael Taylor did not invent the tree." But, of course, California designers Mimi London and Michael Taylor did reinvent the tree with their big tree-trunk furniture.

I caught the West Coast fever in the late 70s when I moved into Olympic Tower in New York to have the experience of living in a contemporary environment. Michael Taylor designed for me an enormous corner banquette, twelve feet by ten feet, to face the floor-to-ceiling windows that looked north to Central Park. It was covered in the palest pistachio glazed cotton quilted in a tiny diamond pattern. The back pillows were big and squashy—each one filled with fifteen pounds of down. These, plus his signature melon pillows in the same pistachio cotton, made the seating the most luxurious imaginable. There was a big scroll coffee table in ivory lacquer. The floor was polished blond wood. Michael had the florist Renny bring in gigantic Chinese baskets filled with fishtail palms. It was California in a New York skyscraper, and a wonderful room for entertaining. (A House & Garden cover, March, 1980.)

So many designers in the West catch the design currents early and invent a few of their own with lasting effect. Frances Elkins was famous for putting usual things together in fresh ways, and created some most unusual designs of her own. Billy Haines set a sleek style for films and his clients' lives. John Dickinson blazed a design trail that delights us still. Now, for example, Tony Hale is bringing the best of East and West traditions together with a refined eye. Andrew Delfino mixes the exuberance of California with the subtle dazzle of his native Venice, Italy. Tony Duquette, a master of make-believe, leads interior designers to look to the fantasy of the theater. He puts treasures from the Orient and beyond into settings that are pure Shangri-la. And why not try for Shangri-la— that beautiful place where life approaches perfection. Interiors as entertainment, as stages for the life we want to live, is very appealing.

Discoveries and inventions give us the raw materials of new trends in living. The genius of the interior designer turns them into something of value. What is the next design trend? This book will help you find an interior designer who will see that you avoid the fleeting fashion and retain the best of the new. The next design trend could make your living arrangements more comfortable, more attractive, and more interesting.■

Mary Jane Pool,
New York City,
October 1991

THE WEST COMES OF AGE.

As recently as the mid-1970s, the interior design establishment of the United States—at the time firmly entrenched in Manhattan—regarded decor west of the Hudson River as being well beyond the pale. Even *Architectural Digest,* then beginning to approach its peak of renown, was thought to emanate from somewhere in New York City, tended by solemn Vassar graduates and sophisticated East Coast taste-makers. General disbelief greeted the news that this glossy and glamorous publication, this quintessential Manhattan publication, came from Los Angeles, city of Philip Marlowe and pre-entree salads. In those days Eastern myopia extended to every phase of Western cultural life– from clothes to cuisine, from literature to fine art. It was enough to point out that California had oranges and, yes, the movies.

It had a great deal more.

Only recently, however, has the country at large begun to appreciate the cultural history of the Pacific Coast and discover some of the impressive contributions that have been made in the area. Throughout the twentieth century it boasted many architects and interior designers and furniture craftsmen of enormous talent and influence.

Most notable in the early years of the century were two unassuming brothers, who combined all three talents. Charles Sumner Greene and Henry Mather Greene are honored in particular for four magnificent "bungalows" they designed between 1907 and 1909 in

OPPOSITE: Tomar Lampert—Crisp marble floors and glass blocks create a dramatic backdrop for a formal contemporary dining area.

Pasadena and Berkeley. Their work shows the influence of the cabinetmaker Gustav Stickley and of the Arts & Crafts Movement that originally came from England. They also shared a world-wide enthusiasm for Japanese craftsmanship which developed a little before the turn-of-the-century. The furniture designed by Greene and Greene—clean, simple and rectilinear—was limited to the interiors of houses they designed for wealthy clients. Never produced in great quantity, it is highly prized today and almost impossible to find. Greene and Greene left an indelible mark on the more modest California bungalows that followed in profusion, simple designs based on their originals.

While not always as innovative as Greene and Greene, many other California architects of the first half of the twentieth century mastered, not only indigenous Spanish Colonial architecture, but almost every past style imaginable; Norman and Tudor, Regency (popular during the 1930s among Hollywood tastemakers), Georgian, Art Deco, Bauhaus—and so forth. Over the years there were many brilliant architects who worked at various times in California: Richard Neutra, for example, Frank Lloyd Wright and his son, Lloyd Wright. There were less brilliant, but more productive architects like Wallace Neff, who in the 1920s and 1930s built a succession of Mexican haciendas and Norman farmhouses, remodeling *Pickfair* several times. There was also Paul Williams, who in a career that spanned fifty years designed more than a thousand houses, houses (when still standing) treasured today by their new owners and contributing greatly to the country's mythological—and even envious—view of life in California.

In addition, furniture design on the Pacific Coast has interested many talented craftsmen and designers, some of them having moved from other parts of the country. One of the most significant was Charles Eames whose series of chairs changed the character of modern furniture design. He influenced Scandinavian modern designers in particular, and after 1941 he and his wife Ray, a painter and designer as well, moved to Venice, California where they produced the famous "Eames" chair, today considered a classic. In 1946 Eames was given a one-man show by the Museum of Modern Art in New York, and today the same sort of innovative furniture design is being produced by artists in Venice and other areas of the Pacific Coast.

It is in the field of interior decor however, that the design history of the Pacific Coast finds its richest chapters. There has been a long tradition of interior design, reaching from Greene and Greene to William Haines, Gladys Belzer and Elsie de Wolfe (Lady Mendl)—among many others. One often overlooked designer was Cedric Gibbons, art director at MGM from 1925 to 1956. He created some remarkable contemporary interiors for his own house in Santa Monica Canyon, when he was married to actress Dolores Del Rio, and he designed the sets for innumerable Hollywood movies. Gibbons is especially admired for his imaginative—and rather fanciful—Art Deco interiors for films.

In more recent years there have been unique and seminal interior designers like the late Michael Taylor, who used natural materials like stone and wicker, together with overscaled furniture and green plants and an abundance of white paint, to create a look that has been imitated and still is imitated all over the country and particularly in California. Taylor was famous for an approach which now has become something of a cliche: blending the indoors with the outdoors, a concept which has influenced contemporary design throughout the country. Take one of his most characteristic designs, the interiors for the *Auberge du Soleil* in northern California: rough walls and polished floors, unfinished wood ceilings and classic antique furniture produce an imaginative blend that has become characteristic of California. In the recent past, too, there have been designers with a more international flavor like the late Kalef Alaton of Los Angeles, the equal of any New York or Paris or London decorator of his time.

Today that long tradition continues, and on all sides there are new and innovative approaches. The gathering of interior designers of talent and vision in the Pacific Coast area is impressive. You have only to look at the pages which follow to find some of their names and some of their unique styles. In their individual ways they are all dealing with the latest Pacific Coast trends: a sincere interest in the environment; an open, athletic way of life; a lively sense of experimentation; a knowledge of the past along with a constructive nostalgia for certain eras (like the 1920s and the 1940s); and the ability to keep well ahead of the rest of the country.

Increasingly stressful, life today has many drawbacks, even in California, and never has the home assumed such importance as a welcome retreat. This is one of the reasons why media rooms are so popular in California today and why so much time and money are spent making the domestic environment pleasant and secure. Interior designers on the Pacific Coast today are approaching these matters with vigor and innovation. Like others before them, they are moving toward the future in seven-league boots. As the major city of the western United States and the acknowledged capital of the Pacific Rim, Los Angeles surely may stand as a symbol of the whole Pacific Coast. It is a city that was, less than a decade ago, considered by many to be no more than amusingly provincial. Today it is an international metropolis of far-reaching significance, and influences from every part of the world—from Europe, Latin America, the Middle East and the Far East—are to be found in all areas of its daily life, not least in the field of design. A clean, fresh wind is blowing from the West.■

Sam Burchell

WORKING WITH AN INTERIOR DESIGNER: MAKING A SPACE YOUR OWN.

Whatever the space—living room or bedroom, Victorian mansion or condominium, sunroom or foyer—the place we live should be an extension of ourselves and our tastes. While styles have changed through the ages, the desire to make a space our own has remained. To try to explain it would be a mistake. But to recognize how natural interior design is to our pleasure, comfort, security and sense of self, is to give the field its proper due, and to inform ourselves of the importance of the professional hand that points the way and leads the way through.

Interior designers are the experts who can help us collect our thoughts, express our tastes, stretch our imaginations, weigh the pleasures and practicalities, and take the best possible advantage of the great legacy of design that is at our doorstep.

Showcase of Interior Design will be your guide, providing the necessary clues you need for finding a designer who is right for you, and getting underway.

Recognizing the benefits.

Initially, when you sit down with the interior designer to talk about priorities, you may find yourself focusing for the first time on what you're really looking for—the style, mood, ambiance. You must also weigh how you intend to use a space. The designer is skilled at interpreting wants and needs and shaping these into ultimate goals. Often there are a number of solutions. The designer can suggest the one that's best for us, while preventing costly mistakes and endless frustration.

How many times have we brought home a spectacular lamp, only to find we had misjudged the scale, were off by a mile with the color, or had forgotten completely that there was no place to plug it in without running fifty feet of cord around the room to reach the nearest outlet? Multiply this single example by the hundreds of decisions and searches involved in redoing an entire room or house and you have trouble. Trouble is precisely what designers know how to avoid: their natural aptitudes enriched by education and experience give them an enviable ability to picture the room and the objects in it. Moreover, their in-depth knowledge of markets, craftsmen, artisans, workrooms, and suppliers enables professionals to find just the right pieces. Left to our more limited devices and quickly-exhausted determinations, without the designer's assistance we tend to settle too easily for what is merely available, missing the prize.

Details are another area in which the interior designer performs arpeggios around our middle-c's. Because designers are highly disciplined in their approach to planning, organizing and executing a plan, they see problems before they happen. We have a tendency to think of details as little gracenotes—things to be added later, corrected or adjusted at the very end. The professional knows better: details must be fine-tuned and executed with assurance; they must be specified up front and completely coordinated.

Nowhere is the adage "the whole is greater than the sum of its parts" more apropos than in interior design. While all the designers presented in our book are highly skilled at accomplishing the parts, what distinguishes them for inclusion in *Showcase of Interior Design* is their ability to achieve the whole—the overall look and character.

A winning relationship.

The process of selecting a designer for a major design or furnishing project can fill us with trepidation. Some of us would like nothing better than to throw the keys to someone else and retreat to an island in the South Pacific until the job is finished. All we need, we tell ourselves, is an interior designer who can read our minds and share every tingle of our financial anguish.

Most of us, however, prefer to be fully engaged in the process and share in the satisfaction of success. To accomplish this we must find an interior designer who reflects our personal tastes, responds to our subtle cues, and respects our budget. Impossible as it first seems, it is possible to achieve this ideal.

While the number of people using interior designers has increased dramatically over the past decade, research shows two primary reasons why many still avoid asking for help. First is concern about losing control over budget, or being intimidated into spending more than one can afford. Second is the question of losing one's personal identity. Designers today are keenly aware of these concerns. Accordingly, they are careful to establish free and open channels of communication with clients, essential to building a basic trust.

Finding a designer who's right for you.

Today there is a tremendous pool of experienced professionals to choose from. While designers may have their own preferences, they generally have the ability to work with a variety of periods. Most designers take the long view, striving for a certain timelessness in their interiors.

Finding the perfect designer for the perfect space goes beyond consideration of style: it takes research. A sizeable part of designer business comes through referrals and recommendations of former clients, so you should talk with your friends or check with professional organizations

such as the American Society of Interior Designers (ASID) or International Society of Interior Designers (ISID). Magazines, books and designer showhouses are other excellent sources. Of course you will want to check credentials, and ask for references.

Here are a number of key points to keep in mind:

ABOVE: Kerry Joyce—A large double-hung window illuminates this cheerful corner, which features bright 1940's inspired French chintz.

Style. Is the designer's work pleasing to you? Remember that some designers have a signature style, evident in all their work, while others may prefer to emphasize a client's individual taste. Either approach is valid. It's a question of what you want, and you must select the designer accordingly. You should plan to interview several designers, and ask to see work they have done.

Professionalism. Does the designer work with a budget and time schedule? Ask about support staff to take care of follow-up work.

Fees. The client should know before beginning what the fee structure will be and have details confirmed in writing. The types of fees are many and varied, and will be discussed further.

Compatibility. Both the client and the designer will usually know at their first meeting if they are on the same wavelength. The designer becomes a part of your life, so you must be comfortable working together. It's important to pay attention to your own reactions as well as those of the designer. Do you feel at ease expressing your likes and dislikes? Do you have the sense that you are being understood?

Choosing a designer is a two-way street. The designer must also feel comfortable with the client, and good designers are selective in this regard. If you are courting a designer—someone you are convinced is right for you—be prepared to address the following points:

Scope of the job. The designer first needs to know what defines the project. Are you planning to redo an entire home, one room, a suite or offices? Are other professionals, such as an architect, involved? What are your expectations?

Style. Is there a particular preference? Do you want to remain true to the architecture, do you lean toward a certain period? You should be as specific as possible about the look you want to create. A client should communicate clearly, organizing thoughts in advance.

Budget. Designers need to know from the very start what the client expects with regard to costs. It is the designer's responsibility to determine if the budget is realistic, whether the project can be accomplished for the money allocated or if adjustments must be made.

Compatibility. As with the client, the designer must be comfortable in the partnership. Particularly with residential design where the process is very personal, the relationship must feel right for the project to be enjoyable for both parties.

Can we talk about money?

Interior designers charge in various ways depending on the services needed. Often a combination fee structure is used for residential projects. Like any other professional, an interior designer must feel adequately compensated to perform at his best.

Design fee/retainer. Many charge a design fee, which helps to pay for the designer's creative talent and time. A deposit or retainer is usually required before work is initiated. This can be treated as part of a design fee or used to cover costs should a client decide not to proceed.

Mark-up on purchases. The designer is a retailer for home furnishings, such as furniture, fabrics, wallpapers, rugs and carpets, and accessories. He buys wholesale and sells retail. The terminology "net plus a percentage" is sometimes used in referring to the mark-up a designer may charge on furnishings. The designer's profit on such purchases is similar to the standard mark-up you pay in a retail store, and goes toward paying his costs of doing business.

Commission on labor. If as part of the design process the designer supervises or coordinates construction and other labor, a percentage of the costs may also be charged to cover the designer's time.

Other charges. Always ask about special charges such as the cost of architectural drawings and renderings; fees for shopping with the client in stores that do not offer a designer commission; and travel or delivery expenses.

Consultation fees. There are times when only a consultation is needed—for example, to rearrange furniture or objects, or to hang paintings. For this, the designer will charge by the hour or the day, plus travel expenses.

As professionals, designers keep track of every hour of their work day and also every dollar that it costs to pay themselves and their assistants. They must cover insurance and other benefits, fund a retirement plan and pay for a studio or office. It is not unusual for a professional designer to spend two dollars on overhead and assistance for every dollar he pays himself. So when designers charge, for example, $60 per hour for consulting time, they are actually paying themselves $20 per hour. This 1-to-3 ratio of wage to hourly rate is common among professions including lawyers, accountants and business consultants.

If a firm offers hourly rates that include all their service expenses, it is a sign of professionalism. The rate may be paid directly in the form of fees or from commissions on furniture, fabrics and other goods and services which are purchased through the design firm. There are as many variations of financial arrangements as there are client/designer agreements.

Long-lasting relationships are based on trust and candid discussions of service cost. A client need not be timid about reviewing the status of budget on a regular basis. Once a budget is established, it allows the designer to seek out economical solutions and to stretch the client's budget to make every dollar count. When considering money, the client should recognize that the designer can offer important savings. The professional has better access to more furniture and decorative arts, and can therefore find the best quality to fit within the budget. Finally, the designer saves money by avoiding the costly mistakes that consumers so often make on their own.

Formalizing the agreement.

The relationship between client and designer should always be clearly spelled out in a letter of agreement. This agreement should specify the services that the designer is expected to provide and the exact conditions under which these services are to be performed. This letter

BELOW: Andrew Gerhard—Creative use of open space combines with dramatic use of color for a sophisticated, functional design.

protects the client as well as the designer, and is drawn up by the designer for client approval.

What is the cost of the average design job? There is no easy answer. A designer may be very happy to undertake a smaller commission that may lead over time to an entire house or to other prestigious commissions. Whatever your budget, remember that mistakes are costly and working with a designer can save you time and money.

Maintaining personal identity.

Most of us want to be active participants throughout the course of our design project. You can maintain a strong personal identity with the project and still take full advantage of the enormous creativity the interior designer provides. The designer knows how to take the needs of the client one step further by offering alternative solutions, and proposing a broader range of choices in fabric, color, furnishings, and decorative arts. Because of extensive training and experience, the designer is quick to recognize opportunities and skilled in finding solutions.

Now the process begins.

In one or two interviews the designer and client get to know one another. Once satisfied they can work together, the focus of the meeting is on understanding more fully the client's likes and dislikes. The designer may ask a client to show blueprints and plans of the existing space, photographs of particular interest from magazines and books, or any other visual aides to facilitate the discussion. Visits to the home give the designer a better sense of how the client lives, what he surrounds himself with.

The relationship between the client and interior designer should always be clearly spelled out in a letter of agreement or contract, drawn up by the designer for client approval. New clients are generally asked to send an advance payment.

Next comes creating a scheme, which is no mystery, provided the designer and client have done their homework. First any architectural or construction work should be reviewed. Then floor plans are developed based primarily on architecture parameters and an analysis of available floor space, traffic patterns, lights, views and the purpose of rooms.

Much research, time and effort go into the final presentation. Schemes are presented on boards, showing floor plans, pictures of the space, furnishings, fabrics, paint colors and specialized surface treatments. This is done so the client can visualize as much as possible. The client must feel comfortable with the scheme and approve the plan as well as a preliminary budget.

Undoubtedly one of the most time-consuming services a designer offers is the selection of furnishings. The client and designer collaborate in this effort, but to save time and confusion, designers often pre-shop the market to keep decisions simple. The key is guidance. Some designers try to condense shopping into two or three days. In certain instances you can work with pictures and swatches. However, designers generally insist that clients see antiques, key furnishings and accessories, sometimes visiting custom upholstery workrooms to insure comfort.

When the vision becomes reality.

The process which begins with an interview, culminates in the final installation—when concepts become tangible and plans materialize before our eyes. This is where the role of the designer takes on epic proportions. By handling all facets of placing orders, coordinating work with contractors, supervising workmen, and scheduling and consolidating deliveries, the designer turns what would ordinarily be mayhem into magic. Orchestrated properly, this last phase can be a grand and rewarding finale to the entire design process.

How to make use of this book.

If you are looking for an interior designer, *Showcase of Interior Design* can be an enormous help. As you examine the work of the professionals presented here, note several whose work you particularly like. Then contact them to discuss your project. If you sense a rapport and compatibility, ask for an appointment to see the designer's portfolio and to continue your discussion in person.
The impulse for interior design has never been stronger than it is today. The number of gifted designers presented in *Showcase of Interior Design* gives the reader an impressive list of genuinely inspired and altogether fascinating professionals to consider. We encourage you to read the individual statements of all the designers in our book.■

ACCENT ON DESIGN

Photo: Murry Kalish

LILA LEVINSON
100 SARATOGA AVENUE, SUITE 300
SANTA CLARA, CA 95051
(408) 257-2588, (415) 949-2525
FAX (408) 249-9045

■ *Good design is good design. It must be timeless, practical, comfortable and reflect each client's needs and dreams.*

My designs incorporate the unexpected and maintain a sense of humor. I'm proud to be known for my in-depth collaboration with each client and extraordinary attention to detail.

Whenever possible, I like to be involved at the conceptual stage so that I can work with the architect, contractor, and lighting and landscape designers as a team to achieve a truly harmonious environment. ■

Photo above: Leslie Venners

Photos, above and opposite: Dennis Burry

PROJECTS:
Private Residences: Private residences and vacation homes in California and Nevada. New construction and remodeling.

Commercial Work: American Cultural Center in Japan; Professional and Executive Offices on the San Francisco Peninsula.

CREDENTIALS:
ASID
Canada College, Interior Design Degree
CKD, Certified Kitchen Designer by National Kitchen and Bath Association
Henry Adams "Designer of the Year," 1990
Showcase Houses, San Francisco Peninsula, 1988-91
Instructor, Interior Design Seminars

PUBLISHED IN:
Sunset Books
Northern California Home & Gardens
Designers Illustrated
Various Newspapers

Thomas C. Achille & Associates

Photo: John Vaughan

THOMAS C. ACHILLE
521 NORTH LA CIENEGA BLVD., SUITE 10
LOS ANGELES, CA 90048
(310) 659-0300   FAX (310) 659-7981

■ *A timeless blend of classic and contemporary elements, related to the client's own personal style is the hallmark of Thomas C. Achille & Associates.* ■

PROJECTS:
Private Residences: Homes and estates throughout California including Beverly Hills, Bel-Air, Brentwood, Santa Monica, Hancock Park, Portola Valley, Palo Alto, and the Monterey Peninsula. East Coast projects include New York City, New York, and Georgetown, Washington, D.C.

Commercial Work: Beverly Hills and Los Angeles.

PUBLISHED IN:
Architectural Digest

BELOW: Diverse elements, including a David Hockney painting, French limestone fireplace and antique needlepoint carpet create an international ambience for a Beverly Hills living room.

OPPOSITE, ABOVE: Space, light and classic architectural elements frame a serene blend of contemporary and period pieces for a grand living room in Los Angeles' Windsor Square neighborhood.

OPPOSITE, BELOW: Painstakingly restored, this venerable Paul Williams estate in Hancock Park includes elaborately detailed draperies and upholstered furnisings to enhance an exceptional collection of signed antiques.

Photos, above: John Vaughan; opposite: Mary E. Nichols

GAIL ADAMS INTERIORS LTD.

GAIL HAYES ADAMS, FASID
110 EAST SAN MIGUEL
PHOENIX, AZ 85012
(620) 274-0074 FAX (602) 274-8897

1820 AVENIDA DEL MUNDO
CORONADO, CA 92118
(619) 435-8268

CREDENTIALS:
Who's Who in Interior Design
ASID, National President, 1985
Fellow of ASID

PUBLISHED IN:
The Designer
Designers West
Phoenix Home and Garden
Phoenix Magazine
Arizona Business and Development

I am dedicated to creating comfortable, distinctive and enduring interiors reflective of the client's lifestyle and objectives. This is acomplished by personally overseeing every phase of design, and always maintaining that client satisfaction is my number one goal in every custom residential and commercial design project. ■

Photos: Mark Boisclair

REGINALD ADAMS AND ASSOCIATES

REGINALD ADAMS
8500 MELROSE AVENUE, SUITE 207
LOS ANGELES, CA 90069
(310) 659-8038   FAX (310) 659-8594

■ *Dramatic, classical style, executed with restraint and an eye for detail. Emphasis on the highest quality craftsmanship and client service.* ■

PROJECTS:
Private Residences: Celebrity clientele includes: Mr. & Mrs. Chevy Chase, Pacific Palisades; Mr. & Mrs. Marlon Jackson (Jackson 5), Encino; Mr. Paul Lynde, Beverly Hills; Miss Pia Zadora, Malibu; Ms. Marlo Thomas, Beverly Hills; and Mr. Jim Nabors, Honolulu, Hawaii.

PUBLISHED IN:
Architectural Digest
House Beautiful
HG
Designers West
Los Angeles Times, Home Section
Los Angeles Magazine
Angeles Magazine
Beverly Hills 213
Orange County
R.S.V.P.
Represented by Designer Previews, Los
 Angeles

THIS PAGE, ABOVE: Residence of
Mr. & Mrs. Stewart Wilson. BELOW:
Residence of Mr. & Mrs. Chevy Chase.

OPPOSITE: Residence of
Mr. & Mrs. Lewis Maler.

Photos, above and opposite: Mary E. Nichols

Photo: Christopher Dow

AINSLEY DESIGN ASSOCIATES

D. DAVID AINSLEY
1106 SECOND STREET, #326
ENCINITAS, CA 92024
(619) 943-8392

■ *My approach to design is a mixed look, working with both modern and traditional classic statements. I studied painting in art school and from there I became a designer. My clients tell me their wants and needs—I'm the funnel and out comes a wonderful paint- ing; the room they always wanted. It's a mystical concept; it works.* ■

Photos: David Valenzuela

36

PROJECTS:
Private Residences: New York, New York; Fort Lauderdale, Florida; Beverly Hills, Westwood, Brentwood, Malibu, Encino, Toluca Lake, Hollywood Hills, Pacific Palisades, Palos Verdes, La Jolla, Lake San Marcos, Cardiff-By-The-Sea, Solana Beach and Del Mar, California.

Commercial Work: President's Office and Lobby, ARA Transportation Group, Inc., Encino, California; Stouffer Lecture Hall, Whittier College, Whittier, California; Moran & Co., Westwood, California;

CREDENTIALS:
ASID, Allied Member, Practitioner
ISID, Professional Member
Parsons School of Design
Pratt Institute

PUBLISHED IN:
Architectural Digest, April 1976
Design House Magazine, 1981
Orange County Registrar, November 1985
Editorial Front Page, "Home Section"
"North Coast Home Section", October 1989

COMPENSATION/FEE STRUCTURE:
$75.00 per hour or depending on the project.

ABOVE: Malibu House

OPPOSITE, ABOVE: Laguna Beach House

OPPOSITE, BELOW: La Jolla House, 14' x 20'

MICHAEL ANTHONY/ASSOCIATES INTERIOR DESIGN, INC.

MICHAEL ANTHONY
SIXTY-SIX EUREKA STREET
SAN FRANCISCO, CA 94114
(415) 255-3066   FAX (415) 255-1968

■ *My personal perspective on interiors is strongly sculptural, combined with an interest in unusual artifacts and classical antique pieces. I am involved in an interpretative process which blends antiquity with contemporary lifestyle. Balance, scale and ultimate comfort places strong emphasis on visual and functional requirements and their relationships to my clients' specific needs.* ■

PROJECTS:
Private Residences: San Francisco and the Greater Bay area to include Atherton, Hillsborough, Tiburon, Ross and Sonoma; Southern California; Seattle, Washington and Chicago, Illinois.

Commercial Work: Lobby, common areas and model, 1150 Sacramento; lobby, common areas, sales office and models, 1700 Van Ness; executive and architectural offices, lobbies and business offices, Taldan Architectural Group; reception, executive and business offices, surgical suite, Presbyterian Hospital; all located in San Francisco.

Photo: John Vaughan

CREDENTIALS:
California College of Arts and Crafts, BA
 Interior Design, 1974
Apprenticeship, Michael Taylor
 Associates
"The Best American Interior Designers",
 HG, 1988
Interior Designers on Parade, San
 Francisco, 1989
IIDEX '91, International Interior Design
 Exposition, Guest of Canadian
 Government
Who's Who in Interior Design, 1988-1991

PUBLISHED IN:
Designers West
House Beautiful
San Francisco Focus
HG
San Francisco Examiner Image
San Francisco Chronicle

FEE STRUCTURE:
The dominant factor in my approach to interior design is to achieve the highest level of quality and design within the budget and project scope. Hourly consultation, percentage on purchases.

Photo, above: John Vaughan; opposite: William Porter

ARKULES + ASSOCIATES

BARBARA ARKULES
5224 EAST ARROYO ROAD
PARADISE VALLEY, AZ 85253
(602) 840-7332 FAX (602) 840-6459

LINDA ARKULES-COHN
340 NORTH DEERE PARK WEST
HIGHLAND PARK, IL 60035
(708) 433-5414

PUBLISHED IN:
Better Homes & Gardens
Casa Vogue
Chicago Tribune Home Section &
  Home Guide
Chicago Sun Times
Design International Compendium
Home
Home Magazine's Best Ideas,
  Kitchen & Bath
House Beautiful's Kitchens/Baths
House Beautiful's Home
  Remodeling & Decorating
Phoenix Home & Garden
The Arizona Republic

BELOW: "God Is In The Details." Design relates to desert landscape and Taliesin architecture. Custom seating of cactus green linen (partially shown) follows curve of linen-covered wall. Base, of same mahogany used throughout, floats, subconsciously widening narrow room. Seating also provides sleeping area. Integrated table/chest at end holds bed linens. Cushions, pillow heights and channel quilting of leather repeat block's 8" height. Custom, curved lighting and furniture restate circular architecture.

OPPOSITE: Henry Moore sculpture sits on custom terrazzo table. Modular table adapts to other sculpture. Terrazzo flooring flows to custom banquettes' bases and integrated corner table that wrap around two walls. Terrazzo's flecks are repeated in bespoke rug. Like black base of Arp sculpture, black silk upholstery acts as visual base for larger works of art. Seating can be reconfigured to focus on concert grand piano (not shown) or to accommodate various social functions.

ASSOCIATED DESIGN CONSULTANTS, INC.

SAM F. TAYLOR IV
722 S.W. SECOND AVENUE, SUITE 300
PORTLAND, OR 97204
(503) 224-1878 FAX (503) 224-6305

■ *The key to a dynamic project is the interaction of the client and designer forming a creative team to develop the best possible result for the client. The process is a great adventure with the client saying where he/she wants to go and the designer acting as a guide along the way.* ■

PROJECTS:
Private Residences: Throughout the Pacific Northwest and Hawaii.

Commercial Work: Hotel and Restaurant design throughout the Pacific Northwest; Corporate Offices from New York to Oregon; and Hospitals and Medical Offices mainly on the West Coast.

CREDENTIALS:
ASID, past Regional Vice President
ASID, National Chapter,
   past Board Member
ASID, Oregon Chapter, past President
University of Oregon, School of
   Architecture and Allied Arts Graduate

N.S.I.D. Award of Excellence for
   Commercial Work
Baron's Who's Who in American Design

PUBLISHED IN:
Northwest Living
Interiors
Progressive Architecture
Contract Magazine
Oregon Business Magazine
Dining Design

Photo: Augie Salbosa.

Photos, above: Augie Salbosa; below: Associated Design Consultants.

AUBERGINE INTERIORS LTD.

LISA ROSE, ISID
256 SOUTH ROBERTSON BLVD.,
SUITE 109
BEVERLY HILLS, CA 90211
(800) 736-2397

201 EAST 83RD STREET
NEW YORK, NY 10028
(212) 737-2397

530 HANDS CREEK ROAD
EAST HAMPTON, NY 11937
(516) 329-0569

■ *Aubergine Interiors combines the experience, talent, and personal attention that can transform dreams and function into beauty and comfort, simple space into a statement of style. We look upon each project as a statement of personality, of mood, of philosophy, and a testament to the individuality and vision of each client. This is accomplished by blending diverse elements from different periods and styles to create timeless design solutions.* ■

PROJECTS:
Private Residences: Manhattan; Select Areas of Long Island; Westchester; East Hampton; Greenwich, Connecticut; Princeton, New Jersey; and Beverly Hills, California.

Commercial Work: Corporate Executive Offices; Private Residential Building Lobbies and Hallways; Physical Therapy Offices; Doctor's Offices; and Private Yachts.

CREDENTIALS:
ISID, Professional Member
ISID, New York Chapter,
 Chief Financial Officer 1990-1991
Cornell University
Who's Who in Interior Design, 1988-90
Who's Who of American Women

PUBLICATIONS:
House Beautiful
House Beautiful Home Decorating
House Beautiful Home Remodeling
Maison Francaise
Interior Design Magazine
Home Magazine
Cosmopolitan Magazine
Home Entertainment Quarterly
Woman's Day
Professional Office Design
Ladies Home Journal
New York Times
New York Post
Daily News
Designer
Home Decorating Ideas

PAMELA BABEY/BABEY-MOULTON

PAMELA BABEY
633 BATTERY STREET, SUITE 118
SAN FRANCISCO, CA 94111
(415) 394-9910   FAX (415) 394-9920

PROJECTS:
Private Residences: Lake Tahoe, Brent-
wood, Atherton, San Francisco, and Marin
County, California; Borlasca, Italy; and
New York, New York.

Commercial Work: Regent Hotel, Milan,
Italy; Shell Central Offices, The Hague
Netherlands; Knoll International, Brussels,
Belgium; and Polo Ralph Lauren, Palo
Alto, California.

CREDENTIALS:
University of California, College of
Environmental Design
Barron's Who's Who in Interior Design

PUBLISHED IN:
Interiors
Interior Design

Photos: Jaime Ardiles-Arce

BARTOLI

DOUGLAS R. BARTOLI
SANTA BARBARA, CA 93101
(805) 569-9212   FAX (805) 569-9214

■ *Since the early 1970s, I have found great pleasure in working closely with clients in creating comfortable environments.*

Houses with charming and engaging interiors do not just happen, they take years of diligent and loving involvement. They should look as if they have always been.

The places that we spend time in should be highly personal; filled with comforting colors, textures, forms and objects that help to recall those times and places that are brimming with sunny memories and simple pleasures.

When I work on commercial projects, I utilize these same values to give a sense of place in history, for in today's world, much of our time is spent outside our homes and these environments should also be comfortable, charming and welcoming. ■

PAULA BERG DESIGN ASSOCIATES

PAULA BERG
7522 EAST MCDONALD DRIVE
SCOTTSDALE, AZ 85250
(602) 998-2344

■ *Creating a comfortable, timeless environment which reflects the client's lifestyle; emphasizing quality detailing and unique finishes form the foundation of my approach to design. I enjoy utilizing artists and craftsmen, especially those from the Southwest, for original one-of-a-kind effects, as whimsy is often introduced for surprise! Texture, rich natural fibers and materials, and antique architectural details, provide an earthiness which is the substance behind my work.* ■

Photos, above: Dave Marlow; below and opposite: Pam Singleton

PROJECTS:
Private Residences: Aspen and Vail, Colorado; Carefree, Paradise Valley, Phoenix, Scottsdale, and Tucson, Arizona; Orlando and Tampa, Florida; Dallas, Texas; Taos and Santa Fe, New Mexico; Los Angeles and San Diego, California; Atlanta, Georgia and Boston, Massachusetts.

Commercial Work: Model homes in San Diego and Scottsdale; offices, restaurants and retail stores.

CREDENTIALS:
ASID, Allied Member
Ohio University, BS Communications
Georgia State University, School of Fine
  Arts (two years)
ASID
Phoenix Home and Garden
Heard Museum Designers Showhouse,
  1989
Phoenix Home and Garden Designers
  Showhouse, 1991
Phoenix Home and Garden, "Masters of
  the Southwest"
Lecturer, Phoenix Home and Garden
  Design Seminars
Street of Dreams, Best Interior
  Design, 1988

PUBLISHED IN:
Home
Phoenix Magazine
Phoenix Home and Garden
San Diego Home and Garden

BLAKELEY-BAZELEY, LTD.

JAMES BLAKELEY III
TRACY UTTERBACK-BLAKELEY
P.O. BOX 5173
BEVERLY HILLS, CA 90210
(213) 653-3548 FAX (213) 653-3550

■ *Our design solutions focus on creating timeless environments that continue to evolve. Clients' needs and desires, preferences of color and style are incorporated into the creative process. Emphasis on architectural details, lighting, and space planning lends itself to encompassing an eclectic group of textures, antiques, furnishings, and client collections. The combination results in an original design conducive to comfortable living.* ■

PROJECTS:
Private Residences: Tom Selleck, Los Angeles and Hawaii; Other Residences: Beverly Hills, Palm Beach, Palm Springs, San Francisco and Santa Barbara, California; Seattle, Washington; New York City and South Hampton, New York.

Commercial Work: Executive Offices of 20th Century Fox, Paramount and Columbia Studios; St. Germain and Dominicks Restaurants; and Sun Vine Medical Clinic.

CREDENTIALS:
James Blakeley III:
ASID
ASID Presidential Citation
DLF
Woodbury University, BS

Tracy Utterback-Blakeley:
Cal-State University Long Beach, BA

PUBLISHED IN:
"Found Objects"
"Sensuous Spaces"
Dimension: Hong Kong
Architectural Digest
Designers West
The Designer
Architectural Lighting
Angeles
Home
Southern California Home & Garden
Hollywood Reporter
Los Angeles
Valley
Homes International
Los Angeles Times

Photos, above: Christover Covey; below: Leland Lee; opposite: Martine Fine

BRADLEY & NOBLE INTERIOR DESIGN

REBECCA BRADLEY

ROBERT NOBLE

REBECCA BRADLEY
297 KANSAS STREET, SUITE C
SAN FRANCISCO, CA 94103
(415) 863-0625   FAX (415) 863-9336

A room needs good bones to begin with. It must be beautiful even when it's bare. We achieve that state by working with our clients, learning about their tastes, personalities and lifestyles. In the end, we've furnished the room together, but our hand is almost imperceptible. We've merely added a little polish to their vision. ∎

Photo: John Vaughan

Photo above: John Vaughan, below: Alan Weintraub

PROJECTS:
Private Residences: San Francisco,
Northern & Southern California; Hawaii;
New York; Massachusetts; and Florida.

Commercial Work: Various corporate and
law offices; restaurants; and
medical facilities.

CREDENTIALS:
Recipients of 1991 San Francisco
Magazine Designer on Parade
 Award
Participants of various showcases houses
 in San Francisco
Rebecca Bradley:
San Francisco State University, MA
Robert Noble:
Fashion Institute of Technology,
 New York, BFA

PUBLISHED IN:
Metropolitan Home
House Beautiful
Better Homes & Gardens
Northern California Home & Garden
Image Magazine
Designers West
The Designer
Designers Illustrated

BROWN-BUCKLEY INC.

THOMAS BUCKLEY
9036 VISTA GRANDE STREET
LOS ANGELES, CA 90069
(310) 274-7652   FAX (310) 274-2921

Photo: Karen Radkai

Photos, above and opposite: Mary Nichols

J.S. BROWN DESIGN

JUNE D. BROWN
SCOTT LOUIS BROWN
3334 EAST COAST HWY, #286
CORONA DEL MAR, CA 92625
(714) 474-9233

■ *The combined experience of 40 years of design brings a polished refinement to this mother and son design team.*

Our design is about appropriateness to architecture, budget allowance and the client's use of the space.

An interior should have an inner glow of timeless beauty, be it a palatial villa or beachfront cottage. ■

PROJECTS:
Private Residences: Laguna Beach, Bel-Air, San Marino, and Rancho Mirage, California; Sunriver, Oregon; Cabo San Lucas, Mexico; and Boston, Massachusetts.

Commercial Work: Restaurants and corporate offices.

CREDENTIALS:
Chicago School of Interior Design
Woodbury University,
  BS Interior Design
Fashion Institute of Design &
  Merchandising
Pasadena Showcase House of
  Design, 1988-91

PUBLISHED IN:
Designers West
Designer
Home
L.A. Times Magazine
Palm Springs Life
Orange Coast
Orange County
Restaurant/Hotel Design
Southern California Home &
  Garden
Featured in Orange County Register

Photos, above: Michael Garland; opposite: John Vaughan

ERIKA BRUNSON DESIGN ASSOCIATES

ERIKA BRUNSON
903 WESTBOURNE DRIVE
LOS ANGELES, CA 90069
TEL: (310) 652-1970 FAX (310) 652-2381

KATHLEEN BUOYMASTER, INC.

KATHLEEN K. BUOYMASTER
6933 LA JOLLA BLVD.
LA JOLLA, CA 92037
(619) 456-2850 FAX (619) 456-0672

■ *Classic choices, appropriateness, quality, proportion, and attention to detail are the key ingredients to interior design excellence. Whether one is designing a traditional project in the pure sense of the word or a*

high style eclectic, the same ingredients apply to achieve a timeless composition. The design adventure should be exhilarating, exciting and fun with the final result being an elevated reflection of your client's taste and lifestyle. ■

PROJECTS:
Private Residences and Commercial Work: La Jolla, Los Angeles, Rancho Santa Fe, Fairbanks Ranch, Palm Desert, Rancho Mirage, San Diego, San Francisco, and Borrego Springs, California.

CREDENTIALS:
Duke University
Interior Designer's Guild of Los Angeles
  (Design Institute of San Diego)

PUBLISHED IN:
Ranch & Coast Magazine
San Diego Magazine
San Diego Home and Garden
Better Homes & Gardens

All Photos: Edward Gohlich

SHARON CAMPBELL INTERIOR DESIGN

SHARON CAMPBELL, ASID
32 ROSS COMMON
ROSS, CA 94957
(415) 461-2353   FAX (415) 461-3813

■ *My clients tell me I listen: I hear the description they are giving of the concept they have in mind. I also observe their lifestyle, and this allows the concept to be translated into reality. When I begin to understand my clients, it becomes possible to put their spirit into their environment.* ■

PROJECTS:
Private Residences: California; Nevada; Oregon; and Washington.

CREDENTIALS:
ASID
Fashion Institute of Interior Design
University of Nevada
Who's Who in Interior Design
Represented by Decorators
  Preview
San Francisco Decorators
  Showcase, 1988 & 1989
Marin Designers Showcase, 1985-87

PUBLISHED IN:
1991 "Decorator & Remodeling",
Meredith Publishing
Sunset Books
San Francisco Examiner & Focus
San Francisco Magazine
Home Magazine
In Marin Magazine
HG
Northern California Home & Garden

All Photos: David Livingston

LINDA CHASE DESIGNS, INC.

LINDA OHLHUES CHASE
3415 TARECO DRIVE
LOS ANGELES, CA 90068
(213) 969-8423

■ *Our interiors are responsive to our clients, and combine the traditional with the unexpected to create elegant and unconventional rooms. Architectural volumes are sculpted by means of color, form, and pattern to produce an environment that is highly individual.* ■

PROJECTS:
Private Residences: Los Angeles, Malibu and Bel-Air, California; Aspen, Colorado; Santa Fe, New Mexico; New York City; Greenwich, Connecticut; Washington, DC; and London, England.

Commercial Work: Time Warner, Inc., Rockefeller Center, New York City; and Palazzo, Beverly Hills, California.

STEVE CHASE ASSOCIATES

STEVE CHASE
70-005 39TH AVENUE
P.O. BOX 1610
RANCHO MIRAGE, CA 92270
(619) 324-4602 FAX (619) 328-3006

■ *We strive for a comfortable and practical setting for our client's lives. We like to work with the architect of the project, whether it is new construction or a remodel and feel some of our greatest strengths are in these services. It is most important to listen to the clients' requests and help them achieve the finished product while avoiding the difficulties associated with building and decorating. Reliability and a good business sense don't hurt either.* ■

PROJECTS: Private Residences:
Switzerland; Germany; France;
Singapore; Mexico; Canada; and through-
out the United States.

Commercial Work: Yachts and Aircraft.

CREDENTIALS:
Rhode Island School of Design
Art Center, Los Angeles
Interior Design Magazine,
  Hall of Fame, 1987
Designers West Magazine,
  Designer of the Year, 1988
Architectural Digest, "The AD 100," 1990

PUBLISHED IN:
Architectural Digest
House Beautiful
HG
Interior Design
Designers West
Town & Country
Palm Springs Life
Los Angeles Magazine
Hawaiian Island Home Magazine
Los Angeles Times
Ambiente

COMPENSATION/FEE STRUCTURE:
Design fee varies on the size of
  the project, cost plus 35%.

Photos, this page and opposite: Mary E. Nichols

Photos: Mary E. Nichols

Photos,above: Jaime Ardiles-Arce; below: Coleman Photography

JACK L. CLARK

Photo: Sheryl Shindler

JACK L. CLARK
202 FAIR OAKS
SAN FRANCISCO, CA 94110
(415) 282-2000   FAX (415) 282-1236

Design should interpret the taste, lifestyle and personality of the client and not that of the designer. ■

CAROL CONWAY DESIGN ASSOCIATES

CAROL CONWAY, ASID
8265 E. DEL CADENA
SCOTTSDALE, AZ 85258
(602) 948-1959

■ *As a designer, I enjoy the special relationship I establish with my clients. I enjoy clients who take an active interest in their projects and who are open to new ideas. Ultimately, the designer must provide a client with service that guarantees availability and a project completed in a timely and professional manner.* ■

PROJECTS:
Private Residences: Scottsdale and Carefree, Arizona; Grand Junction and Aspen, Colorado.

Commercial Work: Womancare Clinic, Dr. Deborah Nemeiro MD, Phoenix, Arizona; Dr. Thomas Hemmer, DO, Gynecology & Obstetrics, Grand Junction, Colorado.

CREDENTIALS:
NCIDQ Accredited
ASID Professional Member
ASID Design Competition Merit
   Award, 1989, 1991
ASID First Place for
   Singular Residential, 1991
Fort Hays Kansas State University
Who's Who in Interior Design,
   1992 International Edition

PUBLISHED IN:
Phoenix Home and Garden,
   February, 1990

Photos; Mark Boisclair

GLENNA COOK INTERIORS

GLENNA COOK
132 EAST THIRD AVENUE
SAN MATEO, CA 94401
(415) 342-5089

I consider myself a designer rather than a decorator. There must be a practical sense to the planning of the rooms and the flow. Whether new construction or remodeling, the house must be made functional and convenient.

The decorating and furnishing are the finishing touches, appealing to the clients' tastes. However, this part of the job cannot be neglected, for the decorating is what everyone sees.

I take great pride concerning the total look, much as an artist looks at his canvas. ■

PROJECTS:
Private Residences and Commercial Work:
San Francisco and Los Angeles, California; Vail, Colorado; Chicago, Illinois;
Miami, Florida; Japan; Hong Kong; Norway; and South America.

CREDENTIALS:
Simmons College, Boston, Massachusetts
UC Berkeley Extension

PUBLISHED IN:
Sunset Books
San Francisco Chronicle

San Francisco Examiner
San Jose Mercury
Home Magazine
HG, "Remodeling Issue"

COOPER/EVERLY DESIGN SERVICES

■ *We are collectors passionate in our search for unusual and appealing furnishings and objects. Our use of subtle backgrounds allows the art and accessories to ultimately give character and strength to the design. Creating rich, warm and luxuriously comfortable rooms that possess a sense of the unexpected is our specialty. We aspire to a finished project that delights our clients beyond their expectations.* ■

CISSIE COOPER
PATRICIA EVERLY
310 ST. CLOUD ROAD
LOS ANGELES, CA 90077
(310) 476-3347 FAX (310) 274-1687

Photos: Jim McHugh

PROJECTS:
Private Residences and Executive Offices: Bel-Air, Beverly Hills, San Francisco and Santa Ynez, California; Chicago, Illinois; New York, New York; Aspen, Colorado; and New Canaan, Connecticut.

JOYCE CRAWFORD, INTERIOR DESIGNER

JOYCE CRAWFORD
PHOENIX, AZ
(602) 952-0080

■ I thrive on lovely things and am stimulated by the avant-garde...by close color palettes playing on texture and line... by wonderful architecture which requires from me understated simplicity...by architectural shortcomings that stretch my imagination into solutions which create a whole new excitement. ■

PROJECTS:
Private Residences: Scottsdale, Paradise Valley, Phoenix, Desert Highlands, Sedona and Forest Highlands in Arizona; Santa Fe, New Mexico; La Jolla, California; Lake Minnetonka, Minnesota; Steamboat Springs and Vail, Colorado; Jackson Hole, Wyoming.

CREDENTIALS:
ASID, Professional Member since 1971
BFA, Environmental Design,
  Arizona State University, 1970
Residential Project Award Winner,
  Central Arizona Chapter, ASID

ASID/Heard Museum Showhouse
  participation as follows:
1984 - Patio & Patio Dining
  Areas in Bill Tull home, Sinquidados,
  Carefree, Arizona
1986 - Red Contemporary Entry in
  remodeled old adobe residence in
  Paradise Valley, Arizona
1989 - Master Suite in Santa Fe style
  Pinnacle Peak home

PUBLISHED IN:
Better Homes & Gardens
Designers West
Phoenix Magazine
Phoenix Home & Garden

Photos: Mark Boisclair

CREATIVE DECORATING

ALLISON A. HOLLAND, ASID
168 POLOKE PLACE
HONOLULU, HI 96822
(808) 955-1465   FAX (808) 949-2290

Whether design-ing for Prince Phillip's Hawaiian vis-it at a private island ranch, developing an eighteenth century horse farm in the English countryside, or restoring a French chateau in Normandy, I enjoy creating quali-ty design with collec-ted clutter and subtle detailing. My strong suit is complicated combinations of won-derful colors, many patterns and all antiques orchestrated in tasteful harmony.

Each area of a room should be full of down comfort and a feast for the eyes–of its owner! ■

PROJECTS:
Private Residences: Hawaiian Islands;
Texas; Colorado; Florida; San Francisco,
California; and Europe.
Commercial Work: Corporate; Clubs;
Boutiques; and Condominiums.

CREDENTIALS:
ASID, Chapter President, National
  Director, Regional Vice President
AIA, Affiliate
SMU, BA
University of Colorado
Parsons in Paris
Baron's Who's Who
Musee Des Art Decoratifs
Guest Lecturer

Docent-Academy of Arts
Garden Club of America, flower arranger
Business owner since 1963
ASID Medalist Award
ASID Residence Design Award
Showhouse Designer

PUBLISHED IN:
Woman's Day
Countryside
Designers West
The Key
Prominent People of Hawaii
Hawaii Remodeling, 5 covers
Numerous other local publications

Photos: David Livingston

DESIGN ASSOCIATES WEST

JUDY A. SIMES
RICHARD B. KENARNEY
101 FIRST STREET, SUITE 194
LOS ALTOS, CA 94022
(415) 941-7880

■ *Design Associates West's charter is: design excellence, on time, within budget.*

Elements required to achieve these goals are education, experience, creativity, innovation, confident and expressive clients, mutual respect and compatibility in the client/designer relationship, an abundance of resources and expertise in project managment.

Over one hundred and sixty satisfied clients are a testimonial to our success in meeting these objectives. ■

PROJECTS:
Private Residences: Preferred residences in San Francisco, Hillsborough, Atherton, Woodside, Portola Valley, Menlo Park, Los Altos Hills, Carmel and Lake Tahoe, California; Orono and Edina, Minnesota; Houston, Texas; Oakbrook and Chicago, Illinois; Saddle River and Franklin Lakes, New Jersey; and Makati and Forbes Park, Manila, Philippines.

Commercial Work: Addison Wesley Publishing Company; Raytheon Corporation; Medical Offices at Stanford; and Law Offices, Mortgage Banking Facilities and Restaurants in the San Francisco Bay Area.

CREDENTIALS:
Major Rooms:
San Francisco Showcase - University High School
Hillsborough Showhouse - Coyote Point Museum
ASID Showhouse - American Cancer Society
San Francisco Symphony Showhouse (Participated numerous times in these showhouses)

Judy A. Simes:
ASID, Professional Member
Curry College - Business Administration (Psychology)

Fashion Institute of Technology - Interior Design (NYC), graduated Magna Cum Laude
Worked with Edith Gecker, FASID in New York. (Ms. Gecker did the White House with Sister Parish during the Kennedy Administration.)

Richard B. Kenarney:
Rutgers University - Business Administration
Dartmouth College - Amos Tuck Graduate School of Business
Publisher, Medical Economics Company
President, Hudson Publishing Company (HOME Magazine)
President, Design Communications, Inc.

Nationally acclaimed firm providing business lectures and workshops to Interior Designers and Architects.
Who's Who in California

PUBLISHED IN:
Peninsula Times Tribune
San Francisco Examiner
California Design
Featured in:
San Jose Mercury News
Designers Illustrated
The Designer

DESIGN PROFILES, INC.

JOAN GRUNDEMAN
DAWN PIEL
26072 MERIT CIRCLE, SUITE 125
LAGUNA HILLS, CA 92653
(714) 582-8550   FAX (714) 582-8557

■ *Our approach to interior design is not unlike that of a chef preparing a gourmet meal. The difference lies not in the recipes used, but in the care and attention given to the blending of ingredients.*

For a broad spectrum of clients, those ingredients include timeless beauty, comfort and originality blended carefully with unique attention to detail. This results in a sense of pride and satisfaction that emanates from our sensitivity to their individual tastes.

We have only one objective: to create environments that generate a special "feeling" when our clients walk from room to room or welcome friends into their homes. Our goal is to ensure this special feeling endures along with the beauty we create. ■

Photos: David Valenzuela

PROJECTS:
Private Residences: Malibu, La Canada, Newport Beach, Palm Springs, Rancho Santa Fe, Various Southern California Communities, Texas, Bermuda and Costa Rica.

Commercial Work: Medical Suites; Corporate Offices; and Law Offices.

CREDENTIALS:
ISID, Professional Member
IFDA, Professional Member
ASID, Allied Member

PUBLISHED IN:
Better Homes & Gardens
Southern California Home & Garden
Orange County Magazine
San Diego Home & Garden
Unique Home & Garden
Ranch & Coast
Family Living
Los Angeles Times

ORLANDO DIAZ-AZCUY DESIGNS

45 MAIDEN LANE
SAN FRANCISCO, CA 94108
(415) 362-4500

PROJECTS:
Private Residences: Numerous residential
projects in San Francisco, Hillsborough
and Sausalito, California, as well as other
cities across the United States.

Commercial Work: Law offices; doctors'
offices; showrooms; athletic clubs; hotel
interiors; and many other prominent
corporate offices in Hong Kong, Thailand,
Tokyo and across the United States.
Designer of furniture and textiles for
several manufacturers.

CREDENTIALS:
Catholic University of America, Wash., DC
 Bachelor of Architecture
University of California at Berkeley,
 Master in Landscape Architecture,
 Master in City and Regional Planning
FACE Award, September 1991
Interior Design Magazine Hall of Fame,
 November 1988
Star Award, Institute of Business
 Designers, June 1987
Honorary Doctor's Degree,
 International Fine Arts College,
 Miami, FL, 1987
Designer of the Year,
 Interiors Magazine, 1982
Who's Who in Design,
 22nd Edition, 1989,90,91,92
Instructor at Harvard Summer Graduate
 School of Design
Orlando Diaz-Azcuy Designs, Inc. was
 created in 1985, with full-time operation
 beginning in the fall of 1987.

Photos: Mark Darley

RODGER DOBBEL INTERIORS

RODGER F. DOBBEL
23 VISTA AVENUE
PIEDMONT, CA 94611
(510) 654-6723

■ *It is through the magic created by the positive relationship between the client and the designer, plus the tools of light, color, texture and scale, that one can interpret creatively and have the sensitivity to reflect the lifestyle of the client. With the addition of quality workmanship, the attention to details and good business ethics, the end results can only be a relaxed elegance that reflects warmth, liveability and luxury. Above all, the design project should be a pleasurable experience.* ■

PROJECTS:
Private Residences: San Francisco, the surrounding Bay Area; Palm Springs, Newport Beach, Los Angeles and Santa Monica, California; New York; New Jersey.

CREDENTIALS:
ASID
Chouinard Art Institute
Baron's Who's Who in Interior Design
Baron's Who's Who in Interior Design, International Edition
Marqui's Who's Who in the West
Marqui's Who's Who in the World
National Philanthropy Day Distinguished Volunteer Honoree Award, 1990

PUBLISHED IN:
House Beautiful
HG
HG, Kitchen and Bath
Better Homes & Gardens Decorating Ideas
Gourmet
Interior Design
Designers West

Photos, this page: Bob Bacon; opposite: Mark Darley

ANNE K. DONAHUE/COOPER-PACIFIC KITCHENS, INC.

ANNE K. DONAHUE
PACIFIC DESIGN CENTER
8687 MELROSE AVENUE, SUITE G-776
WEST HOLLYWOOD, CA 90069
(310) 659-6147

■ *My kitchens are designed for the people who live in them—each project is individual. I use a design approach which incorporates function and the client's needs, based on their lifestyle; I am influenced by simple, straightforward design elements, with an emphasis on natural materials and attention to detail.* ■

PROJECTS:
Private Residences: Los Angeles, Bel Air, Beverly Hills, Malibu, Palm Springs, Montecito, Santa Barbara and La Jolla, California; Aspen, Vail and Denver, Colorado; Scottsdale, Arizona; Las Vegas, Nevada; Tokyo, Japan; Mexico City; and Banff, Canada.

CREDENTIALS:
ASID
IFDA, Current Vice President, Ways and Means
University of Arizona, BS
Royal Academy of Architecture, Copenhagen, Denmark, 1981
Pasadena Showcase House of Design
Calabasas Showcase House of Design
ASID Showcase, "Todd Hunter Mansion" Denver, CO
Judge: Dupont Corian Design Competition, 1991

PUBLISHED IN:
Home Magazine, 5/90, 10/90, 8/91
Designers West, 4/90
Southern California Home & Garden, 5/90
Pasadena Daily Star, 5/90
Valley Magazine, 9/89
"The Best of Kitchen and Bath Designs"
Local Publications

Photos, above: Grey Crawford; below: Joey Terrill; opposite, Grey Crawford.

DOUGLAS ASSOCIATES, INC.

MELINDA S. DOUGLAS
1775 SHERMAN STREET, SUITE 1355
DENVER, CO 80203-4316
(303) 830-0998 FAX (303) 832-6048

3216 FILLMORE STREET
SAN FRANCISCO, CA 94123
(415) 567-1700

■ *The most impor-
tant quality that
a decorator and client
share is the joy in-
herent in the creative
process.*

*What we initiate
together is a voyage
of discovery; of styles,
color and texture
with a mind toward
warmth and elegant
simplicity.*

*I'm a traditionalist.
Family heirlooms, old
books, photographs,
garden flowers and
mementos underscore
the uniqueness of
family and place.*

*Comfort must blend
those special objects
with glorious design,
wonderful fabrics,
antiques and paint-
ings which result in a
fresh perspective in
the client's life.*

*Decisions should
always be shared.*

*Equally important
is that financial trust
is shared. Clients must
know all questions are
treated with respect
and that answers are
responsive.*

*Like the rooms we
decorate, our relation-
ship should evolve,
grow and ultimately,
stand the test of
time.* ■

PROJECTS:
Private Residences: Northern and Southern
California; Idaho; and Illinois.

CREDENTIALS:
Reid Hall, Paris, France
Wells College, BA
CBS-CTS
Carole Mitchell Interiors

Photos, this page: David Livingston; opposite: Mark Sinclair

Photos: David Livingston

DOVETAIL, INC./CONNIE BRITELL

CONNIE BRITELL
7437 WOODROW WILSON DRIVE
LOS ANGELES, CA 90046
(213) 933-8992

1411 LONGFELLOW STREET NW
WASHINGTON, DC 20011
(202) 291-3487

Discovering one's own style, I believe, is simply a matter of asking one vital question: "Who am I trying to please?"

As a designer, I join with my client in stretching to discern and create that personal environment— whether practical or fanciful. My basic design premise: "If I could do anything I want with this room, what would it be?"

In the long run, if you're going to the trouble of decorating, have fun with it— enjoy it. ∎

PROJECTS:
Private Residences: Washington, DC; Boston, Massachusetts; Charleston, South Carolina; New York, New York; Los Angeles and San Francisco, California; Mexico City, Mexico; and the Caribbean.

Commercial Work: Country clubs; hotels and corporate headquarters; law and medical offices; trade showrooms; universities; and historic restoration.

CREDENTIALS:
The College of William and Mary
Harvard Graduate School of Design
National Symphony Orchestra
  Showhouse, Washington, DC
Represented by Designer Previews,
  Washington, DC

PUBLISHED IN:
Boston Globe
Home
Southern Accents
Washington Business News
Washington Post

LANGUAGES ACCOMMODATED:
Japanese and Spanish

Photos: Gordon Beall

LOIS C. ESFORMES INTERIOR DESIGN, INC.

LOIS C. ESFORMES
101 S. ROBERTSON BLVD., #213
LOS ANGELES, CA 90048
(310) 278-2252   FAX (310) 278-2326

PROJECTS:
Private Residences: California; Nevada;
Arizona; Kentucky; New York; Colorado;
and Florida.

Commercial Work: California and
New York.

CREDENTIALS:
University of Arizona, School of Fine Arts
New York School of Interior Design
UCLA, School of Interior Design
Divine Design/Angel Food Project,
  Los Angeles, 1991

Photos: Jeremy Samuelson

EST EST, INC.

TONY SUTTON, ALLIED MEMBER OF ASID
7050 MAIN STREET
SCOTTSDALE, AZ 85251-4314
(602) 946-6555 FAX (602) 423-1093

■ *The key component to a successful designer/client relationship is flexibility, supported by the professional skills and integrity that all design firms can be expected to provide.*

There is always more than one successful solution to every project. That is why interaction with the client is imperative. Upon completion, the project stands on its own as a reflection of the client's individual personality and lifestyle.

As a design firm, EST EST, Inc. defies typecasting. We work on a wide range of project types and styles—often getting involved in the early architectural design stage. ■

Photo: Tony Hernandez

PROJECTS:
Private Residences: Arizona; California; Colorado; Georgia; Idaho; New Mexico; Pennsylvania; Texas; Virginia; and Wyoming.

Commercial Work: Restaurants; resorts; retail stores; and executive, medical and law offices.

CREDENTIALS:
ASID, Allied Member
University of Illinois, BS, Interior Design
Who's Who in Interior Design
  International
Who's Who in the World
Guest Host: Masters of the Southwest
  Seminar, 2 years
Mame Award: Best Interior Design

PUBLISHED IN:
Unique Homes
Vacation Ranches
Phoenix Home & Garden
Hotel and Restaurant Design
Architectural Digest
Interior Design

Photo above: Mark Boisclair, below: Tony Hernandez

EVERAGE DESIGN ALLIANCE

KRISTA J. EVERAGE
JOHN C. EVERAGE
909 LUCILLE AVENUE
VENICE, CA 90291
(310) 301-0010   FAX (310) 822-5526

With respect for the existing architecture, we create interiors in the same manner that an artist approaches a painting or a sculpture; our palette is comprised of color, texture, form, light and space. The style and emotion of those elements are arrived at through a collaboration with the client, who selects us for our personal service and ability to combine aesthetics with function and comfort. Our interiors are liveable, yet elegant, and as casual or formal as the client desires. ■

Photo: Mary E. Nichols

PROJECTS:
Private Residences: Malibu, Pacific Palisades, Brentwood, Bel Air and Beverly Hills, California; and Denver, Colorado.

Commercial Work: Coogie's Beach Cafe, Malibu; Janss Corporation mixed use development, Santa Monica; and various Retail Shops in Los Angeles area.

CREDENTIALS:
University of Cincinnati, BS, School of Architecture and Interior Design

School of the Art Institute of Chicago, MFA
University of Cincinnati, BFA, School of Art

PUBLISHED IN:
Architectural Digest
Sunset
Angeles
Southern California Home & Garden

COMPENSATION/FEE STRUCTURE
Design Fee/Net Plus Percentage

Photos, above: Tim Street-Porter; below: Mary E. Nichols

LINDA L. FLOYD, INC.

LINDA FLOYD
2 HENRY ADAMS STREET, M 50
SAN FRANCISCO, CA 94103
(415) 621-6756

■ *Achieving a time-less and aesthetic reflection of my clients'* *individual personal-ities and lifestyles is the hallmark of my firm's success.*

Inspired by the 18th century's pride in workmanship, quality materials and uncom-promising attention to detail, my work strikes a balance be-tween classical European elegance and our American demand for comfort. My most successful projects have evolved *from a close working relationship with the client, resulting in a welcoming space that has a respect for the surrounding architec-ture and a sense of permanence, continu-ity and style.* ■

PROJECTS:
Private Residences: San Francisco, Piedmont, Hillsborough, Atherton, Portola Valley, Saratoga, Los Gatos, Carmel Valley, Palm Desert, and Sacramento, California and Lake Tahoe, Nevada.

Commercial Work: Corporate offices of Perini Land and Development, Rincon Center San Francisco; The Inn at Depot Hill, Capitola; and various professional offices of residential clients.

CREDENTIALS:
ASID, Allied Member
FIDER Accredited Degree/Interior Design
 San Jose State University
West Valley College
DIFFA Showhouse, San Francisco
House Beautiful Top Ten Best Showhouse
 Rooms Competition
Award of Excellence
Architectural Woodwork Institute

PUBLISHED IN:
Country Inns, Cover
Northern California Home and Garden
Home, Cover
Design Solutions
West Magazine
San Jose Mercury News
ABC/TV Documentary
 "Project Dream House"

Photo above: Ron Starr

DANIELLE GARR DESIGNS

DANIELLE GARR
1811 SIRRINE DRIVE
SANTA ANA, CA 92705
(714) 544-1285 FAX (714) 544-1288

■ *I believe the interior of one's dwelling should re-create the interior of one's mind. A truly sensitive designer will amass a considerable amount of personal history, preferences, and feelings from the client; then combine them using as much insight and empathy as one can elicit in recommending the parameters and details for each individual pro-ject. This skill only evolves from exper-ience. When conscien-tiously applied, the final personalization of the design is brought about with the use of dynamic lighting and the choice of perfect accessories, ultimately creating the client's own custom and unique interior.* ■

Photos: Joyce Young /Buchner & Young Photography, Inc.

CREDENTIALS:
UCLA, BA, Cum Laude
California State University, Los Angeles,
  Masters Program
Cleveland Institute of Art
University of California, Irvine,
  School of Environmental and Interior
  Design

PUBLISHED IN:
Palm Springs Life
Los Angeles Magazine
Orange County Magazine

Garrett Galleries

MARK R. GARRETT, A.S.I.D.
DR. MARIO ENRIQUE MARTINEZ

"VILLAMAR"
LOMAS DEL MAR, #31
FRACC. CLUB DEPORTIVO
ACAPULCO, GRO. 39690

ACAPULCO, MEXICO
52-748-1-2727

■ *Within the nurturing enviroment of sensuous Acapulco, in the beautiful "Villamar", Mark R. Garrett, interior designer and* Dr. Mario Enrique Martinez, neuropsychologist, meet with a select clientele who seek the experience of a psychoaesthetic environment.

Applying ancient Chinese principles that evaluate harmony in dwellings and state of the art neuropsychology, a comprehensive assessment determines the psychological and aesthetic demands of the client's environment. Involving the senses in environmental decisions creates a feeling that home is an extension of one's personality. Thus, decisions are made based on the client's propensities rather than on preconceived aesthetics. ■

Photos: Terry Tomlin

CREDENTIALS:
ASID
PhD
Baylor University
University of Tennessee
University of Madrid, Spain
Vanderbilt University
Lacoste School, Provence, France

PUBLISHED IN:
National Geographic
Southern Living
Sarasota Almanac
Sarasota Magazine
Palm Springs Life
Audio/Visual Interiors
Antiques & Fine Art
Designers West
Nashville Banner

Confrerie de la Chaine des Rotisseurs
Zeitschrift fur Verfahren Humanistischer
  Psycholofie and Padagogik
A review of the Covert Modeling Literature
Journal of Offender Counseling, Services
  and Rehabilitation

GEIER GOODMAN INTERIORS

SUSAN GEIER
3155 VIA DE CABALLO
ENCINITAS, CA 92024
(619) 756-9616

█ *Decorating is the conceptual changing of space into designed living.*

Like a fine painting, it can be bold and vivid or convey a soft subtlety to functional form. Where one client may see a panorama of sand, another may see a painted desert. Each presents a new challenge for us to fulfill their visions.

In California, the quality and style of life is easy going luxury. The convergence of land and seascape with interiors creates that spirit of relaxed living and establishes a reality of purpose for each of our clients.

Elizabeth Barrett Browning possibly summed up our feelings about design and our clients with her oft quoted line "How do I love thee, let me count the ways" and we believe all our clients have the hearts of poets. ■

PROJECTS:
Private Residences: Rancho Santa Fe, Fairbanks Ranch, San Marino, St. Malo and Arrowhead, California; and Oklahoma City, Oklahoma.

Commercial Work: Stock brokerage firms; banks; California and Oklahoma City.

CREDENTIALS:
ASID, Allied Member
Mesa College
Board of Directors, Mesa College
 Design Group, ISID
Educational Awareness, Design
 Center South, 1989 & 1990

PUBLISHED IN:
Designers West
San Diego Business Journal
Thomas Carpets - National
 Advertising Brochure

All Photos: George Kosta

DAVID F. GENTRY DESIGNER/DECORATOR

■ *Each project is as individual as the client...together we can do great things.* ■

PROJECTS:
Private Residences: San Francisco, Hillsborough, Portola Valley, Marin County, and San Joaquin Valley, California; and New Orleans, Louisiana.

Commercial Work: Pacific Heights Place, San Francisco; The Krug Hotels, San Francisco; Sonoma and Healdsburg; Pacific Eastern Real Estate Group located in San Francisco and Bellevue, Washington.

CREDENTIALS:
Celebrating three decades in the design industry

PUBLISHED IN:
Interior Design
Designers West
Better Homes and Gardens
  Decorating Ideas
Northern California Home & Garden

DAVID F. GENTRY
PIER 33 NORTH
SAN FRANCISCO, CA 94111
(415) 956-1752

Photos, above: Stone & Steccati, opposite: David Livingston

GERHARD DESIGN GROUP

ANDREW H. GERHARD, ASID
7630 EL CAMINO REAL
RANCHO LA COSTA, CA 92009
(619) 436-0181   FAX (619) 436-7945

■ *Good design, be it residential or commercial, begins with a good room. The architectural details are always my first consideration in designing an interior.*

Then I work at combining the shapes, forms and elements of that space into an interior that has perfect balance and total livability. ■

Photos: Kim Brun

GERHARD DESIGN GROUP, CONTINUED

PROJECTS:
Private Residences: Beverly Hills,
Malibu, Palm Springs, La Jolla, La Costa,
Rancho Santa Fe, Del Mar, California; Sun
Valley, Idaho; Denver, Colorado; Chicago,
Illinois; St. Louis, Missouri; New York,
New York; Mexico; Brazil; and Canada.

Commercial Work: Headquarters of
Prime Ticket Cable Sports Network,
Los Angeles, California; Cablevision,
Carlsbad, California; Daniels Communica-
tions, Inc., Denver, Colorado; additional
corporate offices; restaurants; resorts;
and country clubs throughout the United
States and abroad.

Photos, above: Kim Brun; below: Mary E. Nichols.

CREDENTIALS:
ASID, Professional Member
Baron's Who's Who in Interior Design,
  1988-92
Advisory Board Member, University of
  California, San Diego, Interior Design
  Program

PUBLISHED IN:
Architectural Digest
Designers West
Business Interiors
HG
San Diego Magazine
Interiors
House Beautiful
Town & Country
San Diego Home/Garden

Photos, above: Kim Brun; below: Mary E. Nichols.

GAIL GREEN, LIMITED

GAIL GREEN
210 EAST 52ND STREET
NEW YORK, NY 10022
(212) 980-1098

■ *My style has been called "Regency Modern," and I think this expresses what I like to do; synthesize traditional*

and modern design concepts to create interiors that have a classical, timeless elegance. ■

PROJECTS:
Private Residences: The Hamptons, Long Island, New York; Connecticut; New Jersey; Beverly Hills; Palm Beach; London; Paris and Tokyo.

Commercial Work: Boutiques; Stores; Offices; Showrooms; and Dinner Clubs in New York, Long Island, Connecticut, New Jersey and Tokyo.

CREDENTIALS:
ASID

PUBLISHED IN:
Casa Vogue
Interior Design
Metropolitan Home
The New York Times
House in the Hamptons
Decorating/Remodeling
Better Homes and Gardens
House Beautiful
Metropolis
The Daily News
New York Newsday
"Style with Elsa Klensch," CNN TV

Photos: Kurt Dolnier

ISABEL GRISWOLD, INC.

ISABEL GRISWOLD
8271 MELROSE AVENUE, SUITE 200
LOS ANGELES, CA 90046
(213) 655-7300   FAX (213) 655-6430

5934 AVENIDA DESIERTO DE LOS LEONES
MEXICO CITY D.F.
(525) 595-4142   FAX (525)683-7696

■ *Isabel Griswold Interiors provide their clients with a harmonious balance of interior architectural detail as well as care-* *fully selected furnishings and accessories.*

"Our commitment to excellence combined with our access to a diverse and effective resource base enables the company to offer a wide range of design services in the residential and commercial fields."

The list of clients includes people from all over the world with the same requisite from their designers: excellence in design and originality. ■

Photos: Charles S. White

GUMP'S

RONALD SCHWARZ
250 POST STREET
SAN FRANCISCO, CA 94108
(415) 984-9306

■ *Our approach to interior design endeavors to integrate the clients' needs to their particular lifestyle. Gump's is a resource that will enable the client to consult with professional designers to combine the latest in contemporary design with the tried and true traditional foundations that have been developed by clients and their families over several generations. We can help coordinate all that is cherished and old with all that is on the cutting edge of new design that will become the inherited treasures and design legacy of the future. The integration of varied lifestyles and cultures for totally comfortable daily living is our goal.* ■

Photos: John Vaughan

WES HAGEMAN INTERIOR DESIGN

WES A. HAGEMAN, ASID
SIX MICHELANGELO
ALISO VIEJO, CA 92656
(714) 588-8213 FAX (714) 588-8133

■ *My clients and I design custom homes and interiors reflecting a common commitment to quality, detail, comfort, and lifestyle. With extensive experience in custom homes, I prefer to be involved in every phase of architectural planning, construction, interior design and decoration. Whatever the style, from a post-modern home in Irvine Cove, to an Italinate villa in Fairbanks Ranch, I bring professionalism and imagination to the project. ■*

PROJECTS:
Private Residences and Commercial
Work: Newport Beach; Fairbanks Ranch;
Rancho Sante Fe; La Jolla; Los Angeles;
Claremont; Irvine Cove; and Laguna
Beach, California.

CREDENTIALS:
University of Denver, BFA
Parsons in Paris
Parsons in Italy
Cannell & Chaffin, 15 years

ALL PHOTOS: Mr. & Mrs. Briggs
Cunningham residence, "Villa Laura,"
Fairbanks Ranch, California.

Photos: Eric Figge Photography

ANTHONY HAIL STUDIO

ANTHONY HAIL
1055 GREEN STREET
SAN FRANCISCO, CA 94133
(415) 928-3500

■ *Although Mr. Hail tends to have clients who prefer traditional interiors, he has successfully completed many projects reflecting contemporary design as well. Mr. Hail strives for a variety of things when designing an interior: an intuitive fusion of quality, craftsmanship, architectural detail of the highest quality, antique furniture and paintings, and upholstery in which soft colors highlight the furnishings.*

The late Michael Greer described Mr. Hail's talents very well, "Anthony Hail is the only designer in the tradition of Elsie de Wolfe. He uses natural fabrics, silks, cottons, mostly off white and beige colors; white flowers in profusion, and a mixture of mostly European antiques, reflecting an enormously eclectic taste, with an overly fastidious eye." ■

Harte-Brownlee & Associates Interior Design

SHELDON M. HARTE

JOHN M. BROWNLEE

DANIEL STEEN

1691 WESTCLIFF DRIVE
NEWPORT BEACH, CA 92660
(714) 548-9530 FAX (714) 548-9528

■ *It is our belief that listening to our clients—helping them interpret their wants, needs and desires is the beginning of a house becoming a home. The design process is creating surroundings, no matter what style, that allow the family a pleasing visual as well as comfortable environment in which to live. From the inception of the project through completion, the result is a reflective, actualized home.* ■

PROJECTS:
Private Residences: U.S. Embassy Residence, Singapore; Newport Beach, Laguna Beach, Beverly Hills, Vintage Indian Wells, San Marino, San Francisco and Lake Tahoe, California; Big Island, Hawaii; and Deer Valley, Utah.

Commercial Work: Pacific Investment Management Co. (PIMCO), Newport Beach, California; Chairman of the Board's Office, Pacific Mutual; Smith International; Nabors-Cadillac, Buick, and Spreen Honda Automobile Agencies.

CREDENTIALS:
Pasadena Showcase House of Design, 1989-91

PUBLISHED IN:
HG
Designers West
L.A. Style
Southern California Home & Garden
California Homes & Life Styles
Orange County
L.A. Times

Photos: David Glomb

Dennis Haworth, FASID & Associates

DENNIS HAWORTH, FASID
P.O. BOX 255427, SUITE #312
SACRAMENTO, CA 95865
(916) 488-7697 FAX (916) 486-8661

My philosophy has always been that my job as an interior designer is to find out what my client's lifestyle, interests and tastes are and to show them how to properly use them while exposing them to other possible design aspects which they may not have considered. It is not my job to tell someone what to like but to show them how to properly use what they do like. Each space should be a reflection of the client, not the designer. I strive to give a timeless, tasteful, comfortable and well detailed look. My commissions have ranged from residential to commercial and contemporary to traditional projects. I enjoy all aspects of interior design styling and put a large emphasis on a very eclectic look. ■

All Photos: Steve Simmons Photography

PROJECTS:
Private Residences: Sacramento, San
Francisco, Long Beach, Palm Springs,
San Diego, Tiburon, San Jose, San Rafel,
Mendocino, Chico, Stockton, and La
Costa, California; Reno, Lake Tahoe,
Minden and Las Vegas, Nevada

Commercial Work: Various office projects; doctors, lawyers, development
companies, and restaurants.

CREDENTIALS:
FASID, Fellow American Society of
  Interior Designers
Rudolph Schaeffer School of Interior
  Design & Color
Twice awarded "Design Excellence"
  Best of Competition

PUBLISHED IN:
California Life Magazine
Sacramento Magazine
McClathcy Newspapers
Sacramento Union

COMPENSATION/FEE STRUCTURE:
Retail, $85.00 per hour for specification,
or hourly plus 35% design fee of invoiced
cost for total projects.

MURIEL HEBERT, INC.

Photo: Donald Jones

MURIEL HEBERT
TONI THURLING
117 SHERIDAN AVENUE
PIEDMONT, CA 94611
(415) 547-1294

Photo: John Vaughan

PROJECTS:
Private Residences: San Francisco Bay
Area, Carmel, Sacramento, California
and Lake Tahoe, Nevada.

Commercial Work: Executive offices;
conference and reception areas; and
private clubs.

CREDENTIALS:
Rudolph Schaeffer School of Design
San Francisco Decorator Showcases
Piedmont Designer Showcases
Hillsborough Designer Showhouse

PUBLISHED IN:
Architectural Digest
HG
House Beautiful
Town & Country
Designers West
Interior Design
San Francisco Examiner
Oakland Tribune

Photo: Jay Graham, Opposite: Fred Lyon

RON HEFLER

RONALD F. HEFLER
465 S. SWEETZER AVENUE
LOS ANGELES, CA 90048
(213) 651-1231 FAX (213) 735-2502

■ *The combined roles of the designer and client today has evolved into a very personal and professional enterprise. My responsibility is to combine the best of my clients' increasingly sophisticated taste with the*

dictates of the job, thereby creating an environment that is beautiful, functional, architecturally detailed and full of the creative expression that each client and commission deserves. ■

PROJECTS:
Private Residences: Los Angeles, Beverly Hills, Bel-Air, Brentwood, Malibu, San Francisco and Palm Springs, California; Tucson, Arizona; New York, New York; and Mexico City and Puerto Vallarta, Mexico.

Commercial Work: Executive offices in Los Angeles and Beverly Hills, California; The Beverly Hills Hotel; Walt Disney Studios; Paramount Pictures; and Twentieth Century Fox.

CREDENTIALS:
University of Illinois, BA
Art Institute, Chicago

PUBLISHED IN:
HG
Interior Visions
House Beautiful
Los Angeles Times
Designers West
Interiors

Photos: Charles S. White

HENDRIX/ALLARDYCE

ILLYA HENDRIX
THOMAS ALLARDYCE
335 N. LA CIENEGA BLVD.
LOS ANGELES, CA 90048
(213) 654-2222

JOANNE HUTCHINSON ASSOCIATES, INC.

PROJECTS:
Private Residences: La Jolla, Rancho
Santa Fe, Palm Desert and San Diego,
California; Honolulu, Hawaii; and
Santa Fe, New Mexico.

CREDENTIALS:
ASID
Stanford University, BA, Fine Arts
San Jose State University, Interior Design

PUBLISHED IN:
San Diego Magazine
Ranch and Coast
Orange County

JOANNE C. HUTCHINSON, ASID
7632 HERSCHEL AVENUE
LA JOLLA, CA 92037
(619) 456-8006 FAX (619) 456-0351

Photos: Mary E. Nichols

VIVIAN IRVINE INTERIORS

VIVIAN IRVINE
251 PARK ROAD
BURLINGAME, CA 94010
(415) 344-2634 FAX (415) 344-2760

■ *To be an effective residential designer is to be a good listener. Clients' lifestyles and preferences give us the direction we need to design a project which is uniquely theirs.*

Communication and honesty between designer and client are the vital elements to success. The atmosphere of trust cannot be overrated as this is more than a business– at its best, it gives pleasure to all parties involved.

With it's countless problems, this is at once satisfying, frustrating, challenging, exhausting, exhilarating, rewarding, and at times even a joyful experience. ■

PROJECTS:
Private Residences: Hillsborough, San Francisco, Los Altos, Woodside, Atherton, Burlingame, Piedmont and San Mateo, California; Apartments in San Francisco; and second homes in Lake Tahoe and Carmel, California.

Commercial Work: Retail Shop and Restaurant, Burlingame, California; Waiting Rooms and Dental Offices, Menlo Park, California; Coffee Shop/Bakeries, Sunnyvale/San Jose, California.

CREDENTIALS:
ASID, Allied Member
Rudolph Schaeffer School of Design
California State University
University of California Extension
Hillsborough Decorators Showhouse, ten years
House Beautiful, "Ten Best Designer Showhouse Rooms," 1987

PUBLISHED IN:
Attics & Basements, Ortho Books
Better Homes and Gardens, "Decorating", 1985 (cover), 1986-88
Better Homes and Gardens, "Bedroom & Bath Ideas",1988 (cover), 1989
Better Homes and Gardens, "Window & Wall Ideas", 1991
House Beautiful, 1987

COMPENSATION/FEE STRUCTURE:
Retainer, hourly fee, net plus percentage on purchases.

Photos, above: John Vaughan; below: Jay Graham; photo opposite: John Vaughan

BARBARA JACOBS INTERIOR DESIGN

Photo: Russ Fischella

BARBARA JACOBS, ASID
12340 SARATOGA-SUNNYVALE ROAD
SARATOGA, CA 95970
(408) 446-2225   FAX (408) 446-2607

■ *Successful interior design is a partnership between a client and the interior designer which allows for the evolution of creativity to transform vision into reality.*

By responding to the expressed needs and desires of my clients, I am able to provide a space for living or working that creates an atmosphere that works for them in all possible ways. Attention to detail, appropriate-

ness of design and a commitment to excellence combine to produce interiors that are both beautiful and inspirational as well as practical.

I have only one goal and that is to please my client. ■

PROJECTS:
Private Residences: San Francisco, Carmel, Los Altos Hills, Hillsborough, Woodside, San Mateo, Los Gatos, Saratoga, and San Jose, California.

CREDENTIALS:
ASID, Professional Member
Elected to Bay Area's Top Designers, 1988
Who's Who in Interior Design
Who's Who in the West
Winner, Project Design Awards, 1983, 1985 & 1989

PUBLISHED IN:
"Home Offices," Sunset Books
"Bookshelves and Cabinets," Sunset Books
Designers West
Better Homes and Gardens
Peninsula
Bay Area Accent
San Francisco Chronicle
San Jose Mercury News
Peninsula Times Tribune

Photos: Russell Abraham

KERRY JOYCE ASSOCIATES INC.

KERRY JOYCE
6114 SCENIC AVENUE
LOS ANGELES, CA 90068
(213) 461-7808

Kerry Joyce's interiors are characterized by a love for detail and fine materials. Able to work in a broad range of styles, he deftly creates satisfying interiors that reflect the personalities and lifestyles of his clients. "I love good design as well as comfort and I take it as a challenge to create an interior that will satisfy both." He believes strongly in the integration of architecture and interior design– having an affinity for both. "I reject trend or fad. Creating a timeless, enduring interior is very important to me." ■

ABOVE: Cream and white beautifully set off a water gilded antique iron bed.

BELOW: Entrance hall with charming antique mahogany child chairs.

OPPOSITE: Gold leafed dimensional wallpaper complement Regency inspired chairs.

KERRY JOYCE ASSOCIATES, INC, CONTINUED

PROJECTS:
Private Residences: Interior architecture and interior design for residences in Los Angeles; Newport Beach; New York City; and Palm Springs.

Commercial Work: Store Design; Restaurants; Corporate Offices in Los Angeles, Palm Springs and Scottsdale.

Product Design: Designer line of Architectural Fireplace Mantels.

CREDENTIALS:
Emmy Award for Set Decoration
New York University, BFA
Society of Motion Picture &
  Television Art Directors
Featured in Metropolitan Homes "Design 100" issue, 1992

PUBLISHED IN:
Angeles Magazine
Elle Decor
House & Garden
Los Angeles Times
Metropolitan Home
Southern California Home & Garden

ABOVE: Gentle colors harmonize a limestone checkerboard floor.

BELOW: Granite and antiqued brass create a dramatic and handsome bathroom.

OPPOSITE: The serenity of white showcases a tranquil grass garden.

DIANE JUST & ASSOCIATES, AN INTERIOR DESIGN CORPORATION

DIANE (DEEDEE) JUST
362 W. MISSION AVENUE, SUITE 203
ESCONDIDO, CA 92025
(619) 741-1266 FAX (619) 741-0499

■ *We are an interior design corporation using a variety of disciplines to achieve our goal:*

an inviting, functional living area best suited to the needs of our clients. To achieve that goal, we combine expertise in space planning, lighting and interior design with client objectives and personal tastes. We enjoy the challenges of both residential and commercial projects, maximizing each opportunity to explore new avenues of design, always maintaining our commitment to excellence. ■

Photos: Sandra Williams

150

PROJECTS:
Private Residences: Escondido, San Diego, Bonsall, Point Loma, Mission Hills, La Jolla, and Rancho Santa Fe, California.

Commercial Work: North County Bank; Southwest Cancer Care; and numerous large and small Medical Facilities and Law Offices.

CREDENTIALS:
ASID
IES
DLF
University of Michigan, BS

Design Institute of San Diego, AA
Advisory Council, Design Institute of San Diego
ASID, Board of Directors, San Diego Chapter, 1984-86
Instructor, Design Institute of San Diego, 1982-87
Student Advisor, Design Institute of San Diego, 1985-87
ASID National Interior Design Project Award, 1988
ASID San Diego Residential Design Award of Excellence, 1987
IES Illumination Design Award, 1987

IES Edwin F. Guth Memorial Lighting Design Award of Merit, 1987
ASID San Diego Commercial Design Award of Honor, 1986
ASID San Diego Designers' Showcase House Awards, 1987, 1990

PUBLISHED IN:
Interior Design
Better Homes and Gardens
San Diego Home & Garden
International Lighting Review
Lighting Design and Application

OPPOSITE, ABOVE: Backlit acrylic shelves glow along their cut edges while halogen lighting accents accessories and slashes shadows across the corrugated wall.

OPPOSITE, BELOW: Handwoven copper fireplace, custom pool table.

KIT DESIGN GROUP

KIT C. LIETZOW
16 LOGO VISTA
DANA POINT, CA 92629
(714) 493-5623 FAX (714) 489-1479

My designs emerge out of an integration of architecture, art, and my clients' personal styles. These elements consolidate in a creative process that yields a product congruent with the space and requirements of any project. I find with this approach that a life enhancing enviromental sculpture reveals itself. ■

Photos: Mary E. Nichols

PROJECTS:
Private Residences: Beach and island communities of Southern California; Newport Beach; Harbor Island; Laguna Beach; San Clemente; Dana Point; Venice; 35,000 sq. ft. hilltop home in Tustin Hills; and a private sailing yacht in Newport Beach, California.

Commercial Work: Law offices; advertising agency; and theme restaurants in Newport Beach, Long Beach, and West Covina, California.

CREDENTIALS:
California State University, Long Beach, BA
Design experience since 1972

PUBLISHED IN:
House Beautiful
Orange Coast
Who's Who in American Executives

ABOVE: Dining room, with American Impressionist painting by Maurice Braun, "Winter Trees".

OPPOSITE, ABOVE LEFT: Powder bathroom with French Empire mirror, circa 1815.

OPPOSITE, BELOW LEFT: Master bedroom sitting area, with American Impressionist painting by Arthur Hoeber, "Moonrise, Hyannisport, Summer of 1906".

KAREN KITOWSKI, ASID, INC.

KAREN KITOWSKI, ASID
2274 BUSH STREET
SAN FRANCISCO, CA 94115
(415) 474-3632

SACRAMENTO, CA
(916) 925-3632

I believe in creating an environment which enables my clients to fulfill their dreams. The finished rooms complement the architectural style of the space and reflect the clients' personalities. Their satisfaction comes from my careful attention to detail, putting their needs and desires first. ∎

PROJECTS:
Private Residences: Various private residences in the San Francisco Bay area, Malibu, Sacramento Valley, and Lake Tahoe, California; Oregon; Idaho; Utah; and Colorado.

Commercial Work: Ski shops; shoe stores; clothing stores; dry cleaners; business and law offices; medical offices; restaurants .

CREDENTIALS:
ASID, Professional Member
California State University, BA
Awards from Woman's Day Magazine
California Council of the Society of
  Registered Architects, and General
  Electric
Who's Who in Interior Design
Feature writer for newspapers and
  magazines
Guest lecturer
Seminar panel member
Participant in San Francisco and
  Sacramento Designer Showhouses
28-year career

PUBLISHED IN:
The Best of Lighting Design
Window Fashions
Better Homes & Gardens
Designers West
Northern California Home & Garden
Lighting Design & Application
Light Magazine
Sacramento Magazine
Peninsula Magazine
Sacramento Bee Newspaper

Photo: John Vaughan

Photo: Bob Van Noy

Photo: David Livingston

ELLEN TERRY LEMER LTD.

ELLEN LEMER KORNEY, ASID
10170 CULVER BLVD.
CULVER CITY, CA 90232
(310) 204-6576 FAX (310) 204-1457

■ *Timeless design, quality and attention to details are essential to creating beautiful living and working environments. An effective designer listens and interprets clients' needs and dreams— designing is a dialogue and an educational process integrating the journey from blueprints to project completion.* ■

Photo: Bill Rothschild

PROJECTS:
Private Residences: Beverly Hills, Bel-Air, Los Angeles and San Francisco, California; New York City Westchester, Long Island, West Hampton, Quoque, East Hampton and Amagansett, New York; and Boca Raton, Florida.

Commercial Work: New York City cooperatives (public spaces); offices, including accounting, law and executive suites.

CREDENTIALS:
ASID, Professional Member
New York School of Interior Design
Parson School of Design
Baron's Who's Who in Interior Design
First place, Residential ASID/L.A. Design Competition

PUBLISHED IN:
"Very Small Living Spaces"
The Designer
Home Entertainment
House Beautiful
Manhattan Living
L.A. West

ABOVE: Sophisticated with its mix of formal and country antique pieces, this charming weekend retreat incorporates cheerful fabrics and Persian rugs.

OPPOSITE, ABOVE: Fine antiques and a pink/green pallette create a warm and romantic master suite accented by a floral needlepoint rug and chintz fabrics.

OPPOSITE, BELOW: Timeless elegance is the tone of the dramatic dining room furnished with classic modern furniture and Oriental accents.

RUTH LIVINGSTON INTERIOR DESIGN

■ *As a service oriented design firm, we are dedicated to meeting our client's needs by designing interiors that fit their lifestyles and budgets, while striving to achieve high levels of aesthetic design.* ■

RUTH LIVINGSTON
74 MAIN STREET
TIBURON, CA 94920
(415) 435-5264

Photo: John Vaughan

PROJECTS:
Private Residences: Throughout the San Francisco Bay Area from Atherton to Sonoma.

Commercial Work: The Chancellor Hotel, Los Angeles, California; Boulder Mountain Village, Sun Valley, Idaho; and La Petite Restaurant, Corte Madera, California.

CREDENTIALS:
University of California, BA, 1974
Golden Gate University, MBA, 1978
Rudolf Schaeffer School of Design, 1980
Marin Designer Showcase, 1985 & 1988

PUBLISHED IN:
Better Homes & Gardens
California Living
Decorating Magazine
Home Remodeling
Sunset Books
San Francisco Magazine
Designers West
Hotel/Motel News
In Marin Magazine

Photos, above: John Vaughan; below: Dennis Anderson

LOWRANCE INTERIORS, INC.

JACK E. LOWRANCE
T. MELVIS LOWRANCE
8465 MELROSE PLACE
LOS ANGELES, CA 90069
(213) 655-9713 FAX (213) 655-0359

Our design style is contemporary with reference to traditional. We believe contemporary design has a freshness that reflects today's lifestyle, but recognize the beauty and richness of historical design. We are as interested in the quality of the architecture as we are in the quality of the furnishings.

Our clients' needs, desires, wishes and dreams are foremost in creating a living environment that will reflect their personalities.

We work with a contract; design fee plus percentage of net costs. ∎

CREDENTIALS:
ASID, Allied Members
ISID, (Jack Lowrance)
University of Texas
Texas Tech University
Wayland College
Interior designers for 25 years

PHOTO BELOW: Private
Residence, Palm Springs.

OPPOSITE: Penthouse East,
The Wilshire House, Los Angeles.

Photos, above and opposite: Max Eckert

LOWRANCE INTERIORS, INC., CONTINUED

PROJECTS:
Private Residences: California; Hawaii; Montana; Oregon; Tennessee; Texas; Washington; London; Mexico City; New York City; and Paris.

Commercial Work: Jimmy's Restaurant, Los Angeles; Sierra Federal Savings & Loan Executive Offices, Beverly Hills.

PUBLISHED IN:
Architectural Digest
Architectural Digest "The 100 Ad"
Bride's
California Home and Lifestyles
Homes International
House Beautiful
HG
Houston Chronicle - Lifestyle Section

Photos: Max Eckert

Los Angeles Times - Home Section
Orange County Home and Garden
    Magazine
Southern Accents
Texas Homes
Unique Homes

LEFT AND OPPOSITE: Penthouse East, The Wilshire House, Los Angeles.

BELOW: Private residence, Palm Springs.

ELISABETH LUCE INTERIORS

ELISABETH LUCE
3476 JACKSON STREET
SAN FRANCISCO, CA 94118
(415) 922-5767

■ *Elisabeth is a traditionalist who mixes a dash of the new and original into her designs. Her inspiration is drawn from color, the mix and match of patterns and her client's personalities and life-styles. Favorite periods include neoclassical and rococo and a strong preference for English and Continental furniture. "I love to create warm welcoming interiors where comfort is uppermost. Layering color, patterns and their interplay, rich fabrics, heavy draperies and antiques (where quality rather than quantity prevails) with contemporary art and lighting for accent."* ■

Photo above: Craig Mole

PROJECTS:
Private Residences: Governor's Mansion, Albany, New York; Long Island, New York; Far Hills, New Jersey; Greenwich, Connecticut; Shaker Heights, Ohio; Kennebunkport, Maine; Delray Beach, Florida; and various residences in the San Francisco area.

CREDENTIALS:
New York School of Interior Design
San Francisco Decorator Showcase, 1989 & 1990
San Francisco DIFFA Showcase, 1989

PUBLISHED IN:
Better Homes and Gardens, Fall 1990 & Spring 1991
Northern California Home and Garden, November 1989 & August 1990
House Beautiful, September 1989

THIS PAGE, ABOVE: An open airy feeling was accomplished for this dining room. BELOW: A welcoming entry hall sets the atmosphere for the entire residence.

OPPOSITE: The living room provides an elegant yet cozy environment which holds a rare collection of fine porcelains and family photos.

Photos: above, John Vaughan; opposite, John Vaughan

MAGNI DESIGN, INC.

JAMES ANTHONY MAGNI
505 N. ROBERTSON BLVD.
LOS ANGELES, CA 90048
(213) 275-2255   FAX (213) 275-1394

Photos: Mary E. Nichols

BRENDA BEERS MOCK INTERIOR DESIGN

BRENDA BEERS MOCK
15 DIVISADERO STREET
SAN FRANCISCO, CA 94117
(415) 626-3808

■ Designing a home or office should be enjoyable. You as a client should be able to explore the myriad options there are for your space.

My role as a designer is to help the client understand their wants, needs and dreams.

Attention to details such as lighting, art and personalized accessories provide an exciting, unique environment.

The interiors I design are a comfortable, personalized, creative mix that reflects each individual's lifestyle and taste. ■

PROJECTS:
Private Residences: San Francisco; Marin; Hillsborough; Blackhawk; Sacramento; and Napa Valley, California.

Commercial Work: Doctors' and Lawyers' Offices; and Restaurants, San Francisco Bay Area.

CREDENTIALS:
ASID, Allied Member
Academy of Art College, San Francisco, BA
San Francisco Decorator Showcase House, 1987 & 1989
Danville Showcase House, 1986

Photos: David Livingston

NELSON, LTD.

WALTER J. NELSON, ASID
P.O. BOX 4130
LEUCADIA, CA 92023-4130
(619) 753-9058   FAX (619) 753-3787

BELOW: Beach House.
OPPOSITE: Private Residence.

Photos: Kim Brun Studios, Inc.

ABOVE: La Casa del Zorro Resort; BELOW: Desert Residence

ABOVE: James S. Copley Memorial Library

OAK INTERIORS

TERRY SHAPIRO
447 MAIN STREET
PLACERVILLE, CA 95667
(916) 621-0471

Whether I'm working on a family home, a mountain retreat, or a large commercial project, my goal is to integrate my client's needs and style into any design solution I develop.

The most successful projects are always those that evolve through a close working relationship with my clients. I am also a firm believer in letting the natural character of a space develop in such a way that it compliments the owner's personal taste and lifestyle. The exchange of ideas, attention to the space itself, and the highlighting of "treasured items" are the aspects of this profession that I love the most. ∎

Photo: Steve Simmons

Photos: Rich Allred

PROJECTS:
Private Residences: Los Angeles, Irvine, Newport Beach, Palos Verdes, Palm Springs, Sacramento, and Northern California. To Mr. and Mrs. Vicini; Mr. and Mrs. Newman; Carl Hillendahl, DDS; and Lowell Plubell, DDS, a special thank you.

Commercial Work: Montevina Winery contracted by Sutter Home Winery; Combellack Bed and Breakfast (published); Street of Dreams 1991, Tree Lake Village, Roseville; numerous Hospitals; Medical and Dental Offices; Law Firms; and Day Care Centers.

CREDENTIALS:
Los Angeles College, AA, 1972
California State University,
  Los Angeles, 1974
American River College, Majored in
  Interior Design
Various Showhouses and Showrooms
  in San Francisco

PUBLISHED IN:
Victoria Home, September 1984
Sierra Heritage Magazine, Winter 1983
Sacramento Magazine, April 1984
Foothill Sierra Lifestyle, Cover 1985
Designer's Illustrated, 1990

P.T.M. INTERIOR DESIGNS, LTD.

CAROL MELTZER
51 EAST 82ND STREET
NEW YORK, NY 10028
(212) 737-5139

64345 VIA RISSO
PALM SPRINGS, CA 92262
(619) 322-0702

■ *Believing design is a reflection of life, I develop a total design concept for each project. My style focuses on harmony and nature and is combined with strong architectural lines. This balance creates a warm and inviting atmosphere, which, coupled with art and antiquities, creates a new blend of tradition and a natural "environmental sense." I like my work to stand on its own, impervious to influences and passing trends.* ■

Photos: James Levin

PROJECTS:
Private Residences and Commercial Work:
New York City and surrounding areas;
Palm Beach; Los Angeles; Ontario; Tokyo
and Osaka, Japan; and London.

CREDENTIALS:
ASID, Accredited Associate Member
Screen Actors Guild
American Center for Design, Member
Fashion Institute of Technology

New York School of Interior Design
Association for International Color
 Directions

PUBLISHED IN:
The Designer
Glamour
The Daily News
The Daily News, "Suzy's Column"
The New York Times
Designer Showcases
Manhattan Magazine
House in The Hamptons

Who's Who in Interior Design '92
Center of Living, NY
Historic Preservation Lighting Seminar
 for ASID NY Chapter,Channel 13,
 News 12

OPPOSITE, ABOVE: Customized table
decoration of etched glass and lacquered
wood adds an elegant touch to each place
setting. Designed by Carol Meltzer.

OPPOSITE, BELOW: Deco inspired
chandelier of mirror and chrome plated
steel custom designed to complement
Lalique table.

ABOVE: "Star-lit" mirrored ceiling custom
designed by Carol Meltzer.

PARISI

STEPHANIE PARISI WALTERS
PRESIDENT & CEO
1217 CAMINO DEL MAR
DEL MAR, CA 92014
(619) 259-0031   FAX (619) 792-8471

 Interior design that expresses international elegance and comfort through antiques, custom made furniture, accessories and art. Ancient artifacts are set with contemporary materials to create looks that transcend time and place. ■

PROJECTS:
Private Residences: La Jolla, Del Mar, Rancho Santa Fe and Newport Beach, California; Scottsdale, Arizona; and Boca Raton, Florida.

Commercial Work: Parisi provides Sales office, club house and model home design work for developers in California, Arizona and Florida.

CREDENTIALS:
San Diego State University, BA and MA, Emphasis on Psychology of Environmental Design
San Diego Design Institute Seminars
Parisi has earned more than 30 awards: Sales and marketing awards for design excellence from the San Diego County Building Industry Association
The Riverside BIA
The Orange County BIA
The Pacific Coast Builders Conference
The National Association of Home Builders
The Southeast Builders Conference

Photos, above and opposite: Joan Vanderschuit

Photo, above: Kim Brun

PUBLISHED IN:
San Diego Magazine
Professional Builder
Builder-Architect
Builder Magazine
Ranch & Coast
Decorating Magazine
San Diego Executive
BIA Builder
Southern California Home & Garden

ABOVE: Casabella. Developer: Davidson Communities.

BELOW: Private home of Chris McKellar, La Jolla, California.

OPPOSITE: Blackhorse Farms of La Jolla. Developer: Davidson Communites

PEARSON INTERIORS, LTD.

SANDRA PEARSON MARTINDALE
5300 NORTH CENTRAL, SUITE 200
PHOENIX, AZ 85012
(602) 264-4227 FAX (602) 265-3590

■ Over the years, we have endeavored to articulate timeless environments as individual as our clientele. This happens when the designer can fully understand the client's taste and lifestyle. We provide a complete range of design services for both residential and commercial needs, giving the utmost attention to detail. ■

Photo: Mark Boisclair

PROJECTS:
Private Residences: Arizona; Denver; Colorado; Seattle, Washington; Victoria, British Columbia; Southern California; Manzanillo, Colima, Mexico.

Commercial Work: Corporate headquarters; law and medical offices; restaurants across the United States and in Canada.

CREDENTIALS:
ASID, Allied Member
Arizona State University
  School of Architecture

PUBLISHED IN:
Orange County
Phoenix Magazine
Phoenix Home and Garden
Arizona Republic
Phoenix Gazette

ABOVE: We gave special attention to the shape of this oil on canvas and its lighting to best befit its space.

OPPOSITE, TOP LEFT: Not every home has a bridge four stories up which lures you to the master retreat.

OPPOSITE, RIGHT: In this picturesque sitting area, even the custom planters are hewn marble.

OPPOSITE, BELOW: This Manzanillo, Colima residence was designed as a getaway. A relaxed atmosphere with numerous locations to enjoy the sunshine and magnificent sunsets.

B.J. PETERSON INTERIOR DESIGN

B.J. PETERSON, ASID
6061 WEST THIRD STREET
LOS ANGLES, CA 90036
(213) 935-3574 FAX (213) 935-5132

Photos, above: John David Hough; below and opposite: Christopher Dow

■ *As a "people person," my design goals are to create environments that please and flatter my client—whether a single person, a couple, a family or a business. The process I use to attain those goals involves interviewing, creativity, research, implementation and supervision. Each step is crucial and is approached energetically and enthusiastically with close attention to the plan and budget.* ■

PROJECTS:
Private Residences: Homes and condo-miniums throughout California, Michigan and Oregon; apartments in New York City; a ranch in central California; and a ski condo at Lake Tahoe. Clients include: Rick & Julie Dees; George Fenneman; and Greer Garson.

Commercial Work: Private Offices for attorneys, doctors and businessmen; restaurants; churches; and television stage sets.

CREDENTIALS:
ASID, Professional Member
BA, Art History
Over 25 years experience in the interior
  design field

PUBLISHED IN:
Design L.A.
Decorating Guide
Designers West
HG
L.A. West
Los Angeles Times
San Diego Union
Media Appearances: The Disney Channel,
  Metromedia, Public Broadcasting Service

Arthur Porras

ARTHUR PORRAS, ASID
5925 KEARNY VILLA ROAD, SUITE 101
SAN DIEGO, CA 92123
(619) 467-9336 FAX (619) 467-9354

When one enters a great home, no one thing makes it great. Rather there is an ambience that creates a feeling of completeness. ■

RAE DESIGNS

MARSHA RAE
FAIR OAKS, CA 95610
(916) 969-2277   FAX (916) 969-2278

■ *Much like a woman who feels elegant in her favorite ball gown, I like for my clients to feel inspired and confident in the interiors we create for them.*

After developing extensive color and personality profiles on our clients, we create a palette and a "look" that articulates their character and lifestyle. The most beautiful design plans blend a client's history, hopes, and dreams with elements that inspire and surprise them. I love to see clients' delight when we have captured their inner spirit and fantasies, especially when they didn't realize they had revealed them. ■

Photos, top and opposite: Ed Asmus; bottom: John Swain

PROJECTS:
Private Residences: Sacramento, Lake Tahoe, San Francisco, Los Altos Hills, and San Jose, California; Oklahoma, Kansas and Texas.

Commercial Work: model homes; restaurants; country clubs; and professional offices.

CREDENTIALS:
Sacramento Street of Dreams, 1987 & 1989
Sacred Heart Christmas Tour, 1990 & 1991
Tahoe Tour, 1990
Conducts numerous seminars and lectures

PUBLISHED IN:
Sacramento Magazine
Kitchen and Bath Specialist, cover November 1989
Sacramento Bee
Santa Rosa Press Democrat
Contra Costa Times
Oakland Tribune
Designers Illustrated
Furniture Catalogs

NAN ROSENBLATT INTERIOR DESIGN

Photo: Russ Fischella

NAN ROSENBLATT, ASID
310 TOWNSEND STREET, SUITE 200
SAN FRANCISCO, CA 94107
(415) 495-0444 FAX (415) 979-0704

In my client relationship, I try to guide rather than dictate. I try to design a comfortable elegance with a definite use of color. I do not wish to impose a personal design statement upon those with whom I work. ■

Photos, above: Dennis Anderson, opposite: John Vaughan

NORMAN J. ROTH & ASSOCIATES

NORMAN J. ROTH, ASID
SAN FRANCISCO, CA
(415) 664-1500   FAX (415) 681-1571

Whether it is residential or commercial, interiors should reflect the lifestyle and taste of our clients. To create these interiors, that are both meaning-ful to the client and suggestive of our design, we utilize an essential element: the constant exchange of ideas. And as always, artwork and acces-sories add the final finishing touches. The end result is a unique and successful design project where the client is comfort-able in their new sur-roundings. ∎

Photos, above and opposite: Jim Peck; below: Tom Savio

PROJECTS:
Private Residences: San Francisco Bay Area, Los Angeles, Palm Springs and Malibu, California; Italy; Spain; Philippines; Great Britain; France; and Saudi Arabia.

Commercial Work: Medical & Dental Offices; Executive Suites; Restaurants;

Project Interior Designer Condominium Complexes; Yachts; and Railway Cars.

CREDENTIALS:
ASID
San Francisco City College
University of California
NSID, past President

NSID & ASID, Board Member
ASID Presidential Citation, 1979
1st Place, Top Honors, ASID, 1990
Design Excellence Awards

PUBLISHED IN:
Designers West
House Beautiful

HG
National Newspapers
Railways of Australia

JAMES P. SAMS, INC.

JAMES P. SAMS
932 N. LA CIENEGA BLVD.
LOS ANGELES, CA 90069
(310) 659-9723   (213) 656-3087

SANCHEZ-RUSCHMEYER INTERIOR DESIGN

CARLOS SANCHEZ
AL RUSCHMEYER
2343 NORTH POINT
SAN FRANCISCO, CA 94123
(415) 563-5477

■ *The design
process is fasci-
nating. The formation
of a partnership to
exchange ideas and
explore clients' needs
brings out aspects of
their personalities that
enable us to create
homes reflecting per-
sonal style.*

*This collaboration
results in homes that
are warm, rich, invit-
ing and most of all,
comfortable.*

*Our work is as
varied as our client
list. Our personal
style? Environments
that reflect a mood
and atmosphere of
ease and graciousness.*

*Partners for over
twelve years, our work
is guided by appropri-
ateness to architecture
and suitability to the
client's lifestyle.*

*Our reward is the
pleasure we take in
seeing delight in our
clients' faces as they
enter a completed
room for the first
time.* ■

PROJECTS:
Private Residences and Commercial
Work: San Francisco, Hillsborough,
Ross, Los Gatos, Lake Tahoe, Carmel,
California; and Southern Florida.

CREDENTIALS:
Carlos Sanchez began his career in art
and theater with a stint in advertising.
He then worked as assistant to the
renowned designer, Michael Taylor, and
was Senior Designer for Macy's Interior
Design Studio before opening the partnership with Al Ruschmeyer in 1979.

Al Ruschmeyer has been in design for
over 18 years, eight of which were in
retail visual merchandising, concluding
with a directorship of a large flagship
department store.

PUBLISHED IN:
The New York Times
San Francisco Chronicle
San Francisco Examiner
Image
Northern California Home & Garden
At Home
San Francisco Focus
The San Mateo Times
San Jose Mercury News
Designers West

Photos, above: John Vaughan; below and opposite: Eric Zepeda

SCHLESINGER & ASSOCIATES

■ *My goal is to provide a unique interior and architectural design service to fulfill a client's vision.* ■

PROJECTS:
Private Residences: Beverly Hills, Bel-Air, Santa Barbara, Malibu and San Francisco, California; and New York.

Commercial Work: Lions Gate Studios, Beowolf Productions, Beneficial Plaza, Beneficial Life Insurance, Simon Wiesenthal Museum.

Los Angeles County Museum of Art & Architecture Tour, 1992
Los Angeles County Museum of Contemporary Art & Architecture Tour, 1986, 1988, 1990

PUBLISHED IN:
Angeles, 1988, 1989, 1990, 1991
Designers West, 1986, 1988, 1989
Audio Video, 1991
Elle Decor, 1992
Architectural Digest, 1992

SHERI SCHLESINGER, ASID
101 S. ROBERTSON BLVD., SUITE 202
LOS ANGELES, CA 90048
(310) 275-1330

Photos: Mary E. Nichols

SALLY SIRKIN INTERIOR DESIGN

SALLY SIRKIN LEWIS
8727 MELROSE AVENUE
LOS ANGELES, CA 90069
(310) 659-4910
FAX (310) 859-8935

■ *Space: Affords the mind time to think and explore; to dream fantasies and envision realities. Symmetry: Invokes the classics and balances the universe. Understatement: Brings tranquility and refinement to our lives. Art: Enriches our souls. Quality: Is everlasting. Design: The sum of the above.* ■

PROJECTS:
Residential; Corporate; Commercial; and Hospitality located in various locations: Boston; California; Chicago; Florida; New York; San Francisco; Washington D.C.; Hawaii; Japan; and Thailand.

CREDENTIALS:
Interior Design Hall of Fame

PUBLISHED IN:
"Architectural Detailing in Residential Interiors," Whitney Publications

"Celebrity Homes," Knapp Press
"Interviews with 20 of the World's Best Designers," Doubleday Press
Angeles Magazine
Architectural Digest
Architectural Digest 100
Chicago Tribune
Designers West
Haute Decor
HG, "Great American Decorators"
International Architectural Digest; Italy, Japan, Germany
International Vogue Decoration
New York Magazine
New York Times, "California International Style"
San Francisco Chronicle
Town & Country
Washington Post
World Book Encyclopedia

Photos: Alex Vertikoff

DIANE SUGAHARA INTERIOR DESIGN & RENOVATION

DIANE SUGAHARA
23 MIDWAY STREET, SUITE B
SAN FRANCISCO, CA 94133
(415) 986-1417   FAX (415) 986-2060

■ *Most of my projects are conceptualized from the ground up with every detail of the environment considered.*

I enjoy creating a beautiful yet comfortable home for my clients where they can entertain and enjoy living. The overall design should be timeless yet always interesting. An understanding of the lifestyle, likes and dislikes of the client are essential to create this environment.

The process should be an enjoyable one for my clients. They are very involved; however, stress is removed by giving exceptional professional service. ■

Photo: John Martin

PROJECTS:
Private Residences: Hillsborough, San Francisco, Napa County, and Modesto, California.

CREDENTIALS:
BA, Psychology, Minor in Art History
Graduate Degree in Education
Advanced Degree in French Cooking
Extensive experience in renovating and building new private residences.

PUBLISHED IN:
Sunset Book on special finishes, 1991
Northern California Home & Garden, August 1991

San Francisco Decorator Showcase, 1991
San Francisco Examiner, April 22, 1991
San Jose Mercury News, May 4, 1991
Fillmore News, 1991
Gump's Catalogue, 1991

ABOVE: 1991 San Francisco Decorators Showcase; pantry.

OPPOSITE, ABOVE: 1991 San Francisco Decorators Showcase; dining area in main kitchen.

OPPOSITE, BELOW: Pacific Heights residence.

Photos, above: John Martin; below: Christopher Irion

HILARY THATZ, INC.

CHERYL DRIVER
38 STANFORD SHOPPING CENTER
PALO ALTO, CA 94304
(415) 323-4200   FAX (415) 323-8300

■ *I specialize in the grandly classical as well as the cozier style of European country. My rooms are romantic and comfortable and never take themselves too seriously. I look for good bones in a room and if they don't exist, I delight in creating architectural detail. An antique or two is essential for adding character and heritage to a room that might otherwise look too new. I like uncontrived contrivance—a clutter, a certain disarray, to make the room look instantly lived in.* ■

PROJECTS:
Private Residences: Chevy Chase, Maryland; Pittsburgh, Pennsylvania; St. Louis Missouri; Portland, Oregon; San Diego, Beverly Hills and Santa Barbara, California; and numerous residences in California's Bay Area.

Commercial Work: PRX; Randall Partin, MD; OSI Travel; Abigail & Co.; Bennicas Financial Corp.; Great America Consulate & President's Office; and The Discovery Zone.

CREDENTIALS:
UCLA, BA
Internship, Keneston & Co. (Antiques)

PUBLISHED IN:
Northern California Home & Garden,
  August 1991 and October 1989
West Home, January 1991
  and June 1990
HG, May 1990
Designer's Illustrated, 1986-89
Better Homes & Gardens, 1991
Sunset Books
Numerous Bay Area Publications,
  1988-91

COMPENSATION/FEE STRUCTURE:
Retail
Wholesale + percentage + hourly
Negotiated fee according to project.

ABOVE: Trompe l'Oeil pediment adds whimsy to this reclusive musician's study.

BELOW: A view of a sunny country house corner.

OPPOSITE: Voluptuous window treatment beckons a young musician to the work at hand.

Photos, above: David Livingston, opposite: John Vaughan

TOMAR LAMPERT ASSOCIATES

STEPHEN TOMAR, ASID
STUART LAMPERT
8900 MELROSE AVENUE, SUITE 202
LOS ANGELES, CA 90069
(310) 271-4299 FAX (310) 271-1569

■ *Good designers, in addition to being creative, should also be editors and coordinators. As designers, we try to understand our clients' ideas, dreams and needs in order to express them in good aesthetics and a functional environment.*

Our approach is to treat interiors the same way an actor treats each role; individually rather than playing the same part each time.

We work in contemporary and traditional styles, incorporating authentic and honest elements. Good design should not become dated, and as time passes we strive for our interiors to become more classic. We like to update past works to maintain a freshness and continuity.

We take pride in our detailing and planning of interior architectural elements such as lighting, built-in cabinets, space planning, finishes and backgrounds. Many of our assignments are designed in conjunction with the client's architects and builders. ■

BELOW: Living room with tropical color tones.

OPPOSITE, ABOVE: Country modern family room.
OPPOSITE, BELOW: Family room provides easy living.

Photo: Philip Thompson

Photo: Chuck White

TOMAR LAMPERT ASSOCIATES, CONTINUED

PROJECTS:
Private Residences: Our present and past residential projects include homes in Beverly Hills, Los Angeles, Malibu and Palm Beach, California; New York, Las Vegas, Philadelphia and Hawaii.

Commercial Work: Executive Offices; Hotels; Retail Stores; Showrooms; and Restaurants.

CREDENTIALS:
Stephen Tomar:
ASID, Professional Member

PUBLISHED IN:
Architectural Digest
Designers West
Los Angeles Magazine
Hollywood Reporter
Angeles Magazine

FEE STRUCTURE:
On Request

THIS PAGE, ABOVE: Living room/gallery for the connoisseur.
BELOW: Formal dining room.

OPPOSITE, ABOVE: Classic contemporary living room with architectural background.
BELOW: Modern day salon.

Photos: Philip Thompson

Photos, above: Philip Thompson; below: Chuck White

TUCKER & MARKS, INC.

SUZANNE M. TUCKER
TIMOTHY F. MARKS
3352 SACRAMENTO STREET
SAN FRANCISCO, CA 94118
(415) 931-3352 FAX (415) 931-6750

■ *Suzanne Tucker and Timothy Marks, both partners in their firm Tucker & Marks, feel comfort-* *able working in a varied milieu. Whether it be a formal house in San Francisco, a cottage on the beach or a fishing lodge in Montana, they approach a project with style, comfort and appropriateness.*

Having both worked under and been strongly influenced by the late Michael Taylor, the designers feel the most important aspect to any project is scale and proportion. They enjoy working closely with their clients, either separately or together, interpreting their needs and thus creating each unique environment. ■

PROJECTS:
Private Residences: California; Montana;
New York; Massachusetts; Hobe Sound;
and Grosse Pointe, Michigan.

Commercial Work: Executive Offices;
Restaurants; Hotels; and Bank of San
Francisco.

CREDENTIALS:
Suzanne M. Tucker:
ASID, Allied Member
University of California, BA Design
University of Oregon, Interior Architecture
University of Michael Taylor, PhD
San Francisco Decorator's
  Showcase, 1988-90

Timothy F. Marks:
University of Colorado, BA
University of Michael Taylor, PhD
San Francisco Decorator's
  Showcase, 1988-90

PUBLISHED IN:
Sunset Books
Northern California Home & Garden
Home Magazine
Image Magazine
HG
San Francisco Chronicle
San Jose Mercury News
The Washington Post

Photos: John Vaughan

EDWIN TURRELL ASSOCIATES

TED TURRELL, ASID
202 FAIR OAKS STREET
SAN FRANCISCO, CA 94110
(415) 282-2000   FAX (415) 282-1236

■ *I like color, both strong and subtle. I like architecture to reflect both time and a sense of place. I like antiques and contem-porary pieces used together to accent each other. I like things grand, both in scale and quality of design. I like things simple both for themselves and to make a decisive statement. Most of all, I am passionate about people and I want to place them in rooms that reflect their tastes, that make them look and work well, to make them happy and to take their place in the world around them with style.* ■

CREDENTIALS:
The Taft School
Lafayette College, AB
Parsons School of Design,
  New York and Paris
ASID, Medalist
The Victorian Society
National Trust for Historic Preservation
Society of Architectural Historians
Designers Lighting Forum
Board of Directors, Pan-Pacific
  Lighting Expo
Board of Directors, DIFFA
  Northern California
Board of Directors, California Legislative
  Council on Interior Design

Photos, opposite and above: David Wakely; below: Mary E. Nichols

Edward C. Turrentine Interior Design, Inc.

EDWARD C. TURRENTINE
70 N. RAYMOND AVENUE
PASADENA, CA 91103
(818) 795-9964 (213) 681-4221

■ *Flawless archi-
tectural back-
grounds are important
in creating a suitable
atmosphere for clients,
whose opinions and
tastes must be taken
into account.*

*It is important to
emphasize clients'
needs, comforts and
dreams; to use their
collections and cher-
ished heirlooms to
create an environ-
ment that is a reflec-
tion of them. Nothing
is indispensable– a
flower can have the
same impact as a
Fabergé egg. My de-
sign is never of the
moment, so that a
project is as current
in years to come as
it was on the day it
was completed.* ■

Photos, above: Jeremy Samuelson, opposite: Douglas Hill

PROJECTS:
Private Residences: From California to Maine, Corporate Executives, Real Estate Developers and Successful Professionals throughout the United States.

Commercial Work: Professional Offices; Restaurants; and Retail Spaces.

CREDENTIALS:
ASID
Woodbury University, BA
Woodbury University, Board of Trustees
Rated one of the top 150 designers in Southern California
Won "Outstanding Residential Designer" Award, 1990/1991 (IF/ASID)

PUBLISHED IN:
House Beautiful, Cover
HG, Cover
Southern California House & Garden, Cover
Los Angeles Homes, Cover
California Home, Cover

Window Fashions, Cover
Designers West, Cover
Unique Homes, Cover
Estates International

DONNA USNICK INTERIOR DESIGN

DONNA D. USNICK
1872 SILVERADO TRAIL
NAPA, CA 94558
(707) 226-9592

■ *Good interior design is expression shared and enjoyed by the client and designer.* ■

PROJECTS:
Private Residences: Napa Valley and San Francisco Bay Area, California.

Commercial Work: Executive Offices and Guest Houses related to the wine industry; Restaurants; Napa Valley Physical Therapy Center; Country Inn Retirement Center; Professional Offices; Banks and Residential Models.

CREDENTIALS:
ASID, Allied Member
University of Wisconsin, BS
Who's Who in Interior Design
Napa Valley Designer Showhouse

PUBLISHED IN:
Better Homes and Gardens

Mark Weaver & Associates

Photo: Jim French

MARK A. WEAVER
521 N. LA CIENEGA BOULEVARD
LOS ANGELES, CA 90048
(213) 855-0400   FAX (213) 855-0332

■ *My career has been greatly inspired by the designer Billy Baldwin—which has influenced my appreciation of both modern and traditional styles. My approach is to combine antiques and contemporary furnishings as they relate to the individual project.*

Successful design is a collaboration of ideas. Most important to me is understanding my client's wants and needs. Then I incorporate these desires with the architectural style and locale to create interiors that are beautiful and unique.

Most rewarding for me in this process is knowing that my clients are comfortable and proud of their surroundings. ■

PROJECTS:
Private Residences: Los Angeles, Beverly Hills, Montecito and San Francisco, California; Aspen, Colorado; New York, New York; Seattle, Washington; Mexico; Piacenza, Italy; Washington, DC; and Hawaii.

Commercial Work: Executive Offices in Los Angeles, Beverly Hills, San Francisco and New York.

CAROL WHARTON & ASSOCIATES

CAROL WHARTON
255 AVENIDA DEL NORTE
REDONDO BEACH, CA 90277
(310) 540-5058   FAX (310) 316-9276

■ *A designer's first and foremost responsibility to his clients is to listen to their needs.*

Communication, sensitivity and follow-up are a must. ■

PROJECTS:
Private Residences: Rolling Hills, Malibu, Palos Verdes Estates and Montecito, California; and Park City, Utah.

Commercial Work: Professional Offices; Law Offices; and Private Yachts.

CREDENTIALS:
ISID
Barron's Who's Who in Interior Design

PUBLISHED IN:
Architectural Digest
Designers West
Los Angeles Times
California Homes & Lifestyles

Photos: David Valenzuela

John Wheatman & Associates

HELEN REED CRADDICK
1933 UNION STREET
SAN FRANCISCO, CA 94123
(415) 346-8300   FAX (415) 771-8652

Photo: David Wakely

Photo: Laurie Black

PETER GILLIAM
1933 UNION STREET
SAN FRANCISCO, CA 94123
(415) 346-8300   FAX (415) 771-8652

Photos: David Wakely

JONATHAN STRALEY
1933 UNION STREET
SAN FRANCISCO, CA 94123
(415) 346-8300   FAX (415) 771-8652

Photo: John Vaughan

Photo: David Wakely

TROY P. WALKER
1933 UNION STREET
SAN FRANCISCO, CA 94123
(415) 346-8300 FAX (415) 771-8652

Photo: John Vaughan

Photo: David Wakely

MARIAN WHEELER INTERIORS

MARIAN WHEELER, ASID
444 DE HARO STREET #122
SAN FRANCISCO, CA 94107
(415) 863-7766   FAX (415) 863-6666

■ *Marian Wheeler's design philosophy is to approach each project studying the needs of the client. Their personalities are the most important things to capture, while enhancing their lifestyles and using the correct elements of interior design.*
"I love listening. My portfolio is as diverse as my clientele. My favorite call is from a client after installation. 'You've really captured me...' this is where I receive satisfaction." ■

CREDENTIALS:
ASID
Art Institute of Pittsburg, Interior Design

PROJECTS:
Include residential and commercial; from very small and exciting to very large brokerage firms.

PUBLISHED IN:
Northern California Home and Garden
Designers West
House and Garden
Designers Illustrated
San Francisco Chronicle
San Mateo Times

WISEMAN AND GALE INTERIORS, INC.

ANNE GALE
7120 E. INDIAN SCHOOL ROAD
SCOTTSDALE, AZ 85251
(602) 945-8447

For 30 years, Wiseman and Gale have been interpreting the Southwestern lifestyle for clients who come from all over the country. We create interiors for our clients which adapt their own traditions and backgrounds to the new way of living. Southwestern style elements come from both the European/Spanish settlers and the native American indians. We translate these into interesting colors and textures; handcrafted and useful furniture; window treatments suited to desert sun; rugged floors suited to indoor and outdoor living—all put together in a lively and liveable manner. ∎

BELOW: A dining room with antique chairs and special needlework seats. The Spanish Colonial chandelier is festooned with dried flowers of the season.

PROJECTS:
Private Residences: Arizona; California;
Colorado; New Mexico; Utah;
Washington; Indiana; and Alabama.

Commercial Work: Professional Offices
in Arizona.

PUBLISHED IN:
House Beautiful, 1990
Home Magazine, 1989
Phoenix Home and Garden, 1986-90
Phoenix Magazine, 1989

CREDENTIALS:
ASID

ABOVE: Living room done for Heard
Museum Showcase House in 1990,
showing frescoed walls, handmade fabric
on sofa, and antique Colonial furniture.

R. GARY WOLPER

R. GARY WOLPER
8451 CLINTON AVENUE
WEST HOLLYWOOD, CA 90048
(213) 651-1416

Photos: Christopher Dow

BARBARA WOOLF INTERIORS, INC.

BARBARA WOOLF, ISID
120 S. ROBERTSON BLVD.
LOS ANGELES, CA 90048
(310) 859-1970   (310) 278-3530

■ *My work in-corporates custom design projects including residences, corporate spaces and hotels, but I have two predominant loves: one for property restoration; the other to have clients with imagination! It's a joy creating illusions, dreams and fantasies that combat today's stressful and complex world...a place to escape and rejuvenate... a place for a wonderful celebration...or a place to simply relax and enjoy one's surroundings. ■*

Photos: George Szanik

PROJECTS:
Restoration: "Pickfair," former Beverly Hills home of Mary Pickford & Douglas Fairbanks; "Sunset Towers Hotel," Los Angeles, home of numerous Hollywood celebrities.

Private Residences: Thai-style home for Mr. & Mrs. Roger McGee, Kona, Hawaii; numerous estates throughout Bel-Air, Beverly Hills, Hancock Park, Malibu, Pacific Palisades, Palos Verdes Estates and Rancho Mirage, California.

Commercial Work: Continental Development Corporation; Dart Industries; Fantasy Theme Hotel, Los Angeles; The Los Angeles Forum; Six Flags Magic Mountain; Sopac Energy Corporation; and numerous Law Offices.

Custom Work: "Romance of the Orient" custom rug series for Chiyoda Rug Company, Tokyo, Japan.

CREDENTIALS:
ISID, Professional Member
ISID, Los Angeles Chapter, Served on Board of Directors
Building Industry Association, Los Angeles Chapter, Served on Board of Directors
UCLA, Art and Design curriculum
Baron's Who's Who in Interior Design, 1990-1992
Guest speaker for interior design business practices and contracts

PUBLISHED IN:
Designers West, "Design for Celebrities" and "East Meets West"
The Designer, New York
Today's Living, Phoenix
The Los Angeles Times Home Magazine, numerous issues

ABOVE: The Versailles Room at the Pickfair Estate in Beverly Hills, former home of America's sweetheart Mary Pickford and husband Douglas Fairbanks, incorporates boiserie and an embossed tin ceiling in 22K gold leaf, enraptures dinner guests in rococo splendor.

BELOW: A serene azure koi pond distinguishes a Beverly Hills garden for casual entertaining or a soothing sanctuary for private moments.

OPPOSITE: An exotic Russian red living room in a Beverly Hills maisonette functions masterfully as a backdrop for grand scale galas or relaxation from the demands of city living.

234

YOKOMIZO ASSOCIATES, INC.

JOYCE YOKOMIZO
435 JACKSON STREET
SAN FRANCISCO, CA 94111
(415) 433-5061 FAX (415) 434-2230

■ *Our most successful designs are those that reflect the philosophies, work styles and personalities of our clients; whether corporate, hospitality or residential. Each project presents us with a new challenge and, ultimately, the responsibility for utilizing our diverse talents and skills to create a unique environment that works!* ■

PROJECTS:
Residential Work: San Francisco, Tiburon, Mill Valley, Oakland, and Sonoma, California; and Glenbrook, Nevada.

Commercial Work: Sonoma Mission Inn & Spa; Sheraton Hotels; Apple Computer; The Good Guys; La Salle Partners; Graham & James; California Compensation; and Kohlberg, Kravis & Roberts.

PUBLISHED IN:
Interiors
Architectural Record
Contract
Architect AIA
The Office
Designers West
Restaurant Hospitality
San Francisco Chronicle

Photos, this page: David Livingston

Photo above: Colin McRae, below: John Sutton

B. Jordan Young Inc.

BETTYE JORDAN YOUNG
6565 SUNSET BOULEVARD, SUITE 318
HOLLYWOOD, CA 90028
(213) 871-4944 FAX (213) 876-1133

A great space is a theater for life. It is important that the production be built around a team effort. Egos must take a back seat in order that function and value be established as efficiently as possible. As the bones of the set, the architecture has to be responded to and respected. Proportion and detail, color and light go hand-in-hand in streamlining and enhancing the theme. Knowing what is not needed is often times as important as what is. Communication is everything in producing a comfortable, almost second skin fit. Good design, like a favorite piece of music, is never tiring. ■

PROJECTS:
Private Residences and Commercial Work: New York City and Southampton, New York; Atlanta, Georgia; Dallas, Texas; Palm Beach, Florida; Los Angeles, California; and London, England.

CREDENTIALS:
Georgia State University, BVA
Guest Lecturer and Critic; Savannah College of Arts and Design
Parsons School of Design

PUBLISHED IN:
Architectural Digest
Interiors
Kateigaho
Interior Design

Photos: Jamie Ardiles-Arces

INDEX OF INTERIOR DESIGNERS

INDEX OF PHOTOGRAPHERS